Fennings Taylor

The last three Bishops Appointed by the Crown for the Anglican Church of Canada

Fennings Taylor

The last three Bishops Appointed by the Crown for the Anglican Church of Canada

ISBN/EAN: 9783337216153

Printed in Europe, USA, Canada, Australia, Japan

Cover: Foto ©Lupo / pixelio.de

More available books at **www.hansebooks.com**

THE LAST THREE BISHOPS,

APPOINTED BY THE CROWN,

FOR THE

ANGLICAN CHURCH OF CANADA.

BY

FENNINGS TAYLOR.

DEPUTY CLERK, AND CLERK ASSISTANT OF THE SENATE OF CANADA,

Author of "Sketches of British Americans," "The Life and Death of the Hon. T. D'Arcy McGee," &c., &c., &c.

MONTREAL:
JOHN LOVELL, ST. NICHOLAS STREET.
1869.

Entered according to Act of the Parliament of Canada, in the year one thousand eight hundred and sixty-nine, by FENNINGS TAYLOR, in the Office of the Minister of Agriculture.

PREFACE.

The Year 1850 will be accounted a noteworthy era in the history of the Province of Canada; for in that year the Royal Supremacy in matters ecclesiastical was asserted for the last time, when Her Majesty, in the exercise of Her prerogative, was pleased to nominate and appoint the Right Reverend FRANCIS FULFORD, D.D., to be the first Bishop of the newly created Diocese of Montreal.

For the convenience of the Anglican Church in Canada, the Province was then divided into the Dioceses of Quebec, Toronto and Montreal, which were respectively ruled by the Right Reverend GEORGE JEHOSHAPHAT MOUNTAIN, D.D., D.C.L., the Honourable and Right Reverend JOHN STRACHAN, D.D., LL.D., and the Most Reverend FRANCIS FULFORD, D.D. Within a period of less than six years all these eminent men have passed to their rest, and, for the reasons we shall state in the course of the following reviews, the function of the State with respect to the appointment of Bishops may be said to have expired with them.

The concurrence of events so unique and unprecedented, is calculated to excite attention elsewhere than in the place where those events have transpired. It is scarcely too much to say, that the changes through which the Church of England is now passing have in no small degree been hastened by the example which the Anglican Church of Canada has supplied. It may, therefore, for this as well as for other reasons, be desirable to preserve in a convenient form, by way of a remembrance, or as a "review and a study," some notes of the lives of three Prelates, who by their efforts to organize and consolidate the Church of Canada, did much to withdraw the affairs of religion from the controul of Parliament, and not a little towards bringing about the events which are now agitating the United Kingdom, and which

Preface.

are likely to fill no unimportant place in the history of the Church of Christ.

The author desires to avail himself of the opportunity which a preface affords, to express his sincere thanks to the Lord BISHOP OF QUEBEC, to the Lord BISHOP OF TORONTO, and to the Lord BISHOP OF ONTARIO, for valuable information procured with no little trouble and bestowed with no little cheerfulness. He also wishes to offer his grateful acknowledgments to the Venerable H. PATTON, D.C.L., Archdeacon of Ontario; to the Rev. H. SCADDING, D.D., of Toronto; to the Rev. SALTERN GIVENS, M.A., of Yorkville; to the Rev. P. W. LOOSEMORE, M.A., Senior Canon of the Cathedral of Montreal; to the Rev. G. WHITAKER, M.A., Provost of the University of Trinity College, Toronto, and the Rev. J. H. NICOLLS, D.D., Principal and Professor of Divinity of the University of Bishop's College, Lennoxville, for supplying him with valuable statistical information on subjects upon which he could not very conveniently have informed himself.

Preface.

This work should have appeared several months ago, and the author can only apologize and express his regret for the delay which has occurred in the publication. The reasons for such delay were of a local kind, and took their rise in one of those periodical derangements, to which all trade is liable, and for which neither he nor the publisher must be held responsible.

OTTAWA, Canada, 1st November, 1869.

Table of Contents.

THE MOST REVEREND
FRANCIS FULFORD, D.D.
LORD BISHOP OF MONTREAL,
AND
METROPOLITAN OF CANADA.

CHAPTER ONE

The Fulford family of great antiquity. Their mansion and estate. Historical pictures. Knights of Great Fulford. The Crusades. Single combat with a Saracen of "great bulk and bigness." Ardent Lancastrians. Wars of the Roses. Sir William Fulford, with Chief Justice Sir William Gascoigne, sent to suppress the insurrection in the north of England. Henry Percy (Hotspur) and Archbishop Scroope. Battle of Towton Field. The relief of Exeter when besieged by Perkin Warbeck. Lord Edward Courtenie, Earl of Devonshire. Great Fulford garrisoned for Charles the First. Surrender to General Fairfax. Later times. Birth, education and marriage of the Rev. Francis Fulford, the future Metropolitan of Canada. His clerical and literary work in England. The degree of D.D. conferred on him. His Church work in England a fitting prelude to church work in Canada. Reasons therefor. Contemporary state of the Anglican Church in Canada. Creation of the new Diocese of Montreal and consecration of Dr. Fulford, as the first Bishop. Church parties in Canada. The "Oxford movement" and its influence. Sympathetic excitement more curious than commendable. Dr. Fulford's contemporaries at Oxford. Canon Hawkins. The Bishop of Newfoundland. The Bishop of Fredericton. Questions of the day. The "Hampden scandal." The "Gorham controversy," and "the Surplice question." Their effect in Canada. Quiet Churchmen comforted by the appointment of Dr. Fulford.

Chapter Two.

Dr. Fulford's arrival. "He is wanted very badly." Excessive curiosity with respect to his character and opinions. The Bishop's governing qualities. Recognizes the value of silence. Silence not appreciated by all the clergy. It provokes curiosity. Such curiosity adroitly met, and cleverly rebuked. Anecdote. Addresses of welcome. Enthronement at Christ Church, Montreal. Officiating clergymen. Anecdote of the Garrison Chaplain. Why "his hair stood on end." Organization of the Church Society of the Diocese. Difficulty with the Colonial Church and School Society. The Bishop's letter thereon. Primary visitation. Speculations of the clergy thereupon. New views promulgated on the status of the Anglican Church in Canada. The clergy enjoy no especial privileges in Canada. Effects of religious equality. New duties with respect to the various denominations. Criticism on the Ecclesiastical appointments made in England by the Pope. A character of the reformation. The necessity for "Creeds, Catechisms and Confessions of faith." Baxter's Catechism quoted thereon. The question of Common Schools. The Bishops of Montreal and Toronto not in accord on the subject. The laity generally sympathize with the former, whose liberal principles are warmly appreciated by the Provincial administration of the period.

Chapter Three.

The Bishop's policy attended with marked results. Astonishing increase of the actual and comparative Church population of Montreal. Temporary failure of his effort to establish a Church of England school for girls. Re-organization of the Cathedral staff. Protestant Parish of Montreal divided into conventional Parishes, or Church Districts. The Church system becomes more Parochial and less Congregational. "Evangelical" system defective in this particular. Arrival of Archdeacon Lower and Canon Gilson. They are appointed to the Cathedral Staff. The former marries the Bishop's only daughter. Elected vs. nominated Bishops. Defects of the former system as practised in Canada. Difficulty of being impartial when chosen by a party. Diversity and not uniformity the law of creation. This condition practically recognized by the Church of England. Accepted and illustrated by the Bishop when administering patronage. His strong sympathy with all Benevolent and Literary associations. Effort to live peaceably with all men. Consecration of the Montreal Cemetery. Approval of all Protestants thereat. The

Table of Contents. IX

Bishop's monument side by side with the monument of the Honourable Peter McGill. The Bishop's respect for religious principle mingled with a regard for human feeling. The influence of personal character. Knowledge without practice deprecated. "Noah's Carpenters." Religious work performed for religious ends. The Bishop's writings. Confirmation Addresses. Extract. The duty of being "all things to all men." Not a rigid rubrician. Anecdote. Cathedral destroyed by fire. New Cathedral. Large Debt thereon. The Bishop's manner of life. His humility. His hospitality. Dean Bethune. Canon Balch. The Cathedral, the Bishop's best monument.

CHAPTER FOUR.

Co-operation and union characteristics of the age. Exemplified in commercial undertakings. In state politics. In religious efforts. The prayer for christian unity the common prayer of christian people. Episcopal supervision a condition of unity. The want of Bishops, the defect of the Episcopal Churches of America and Canada. The increase of the Colonial Episcopate, one of the first fruits of the Oxford movement. Parishes gathered into Dioceses. Dioceses gathered into Provinces. Synodical action. Energetic proceedings of the Bishop of Toronto thereon. Imitated by the Bishop of Quebec. Meeting of the Bishops at Quebec. A canon on convocation adopted. Failure of proceedings relating thereto in the British Parliament. Their success in the Canadian Legislature. Bill thereon passed. Canadian Dioceses assembled in Provincial Synod. Petition for the appointment of a Metropolitan. Right Rev. Francis Fulford appointed. Fraternal address to the Protestant Episcopal Church in the United States. Metropolitan of Canada preaches before the Protestant Episcopal convocation of the United States at Philadelphia. Present at the consecration of the Right Rev. Bishop Wainwright, and at the consecration of the Right Reverend Horatio Potter. Exertions to bring about a closer union between the Canadian and American Churches. Consecration of the Bishops of Ontario and Quebec. The Bishop of Michigan. The Bishop of Vermont. No more Royal Mandates for the consecration of Canadian Bishops to be issued. The practical effect of such an order. Independence of the Anglican Church in Canada. Efforts to obliterate the red line of blood which separates the Canadian and American people. Keble's hymn on Unity.

Table of Contents.

CHAPTER FIVE.

Triennial meeting of the Provincial Synod, and address to the Archbishop of Canterbury to convene a National Synod of the Anglican Church. The Bishop of Ontario. Answer of the Archbishop of Canterbury. The Lambeth conference a result of the action of the Canadian Church. The Bishop of Illinois thereon. The grave duties which the Conference imposed on the Canadian Metropolitan. His return to Canada. Presides at the Diocesan Synod. His opinion of the Lambeth Conference. Attends the annual convocation of the university of Bishop's College. Visits the Deanery of St. Andrews. Holds confirmation services. Remarks of the Rev. Canon Loosemore thereon. Returns to Montreal to meet the Provincial Synod. Dies the day after the Provincial Synod assembled. The Metropolitan's opinions on the ritualistic controversy. Reflections thereon. The Bishop's reticence. Rarely praised or blamed any one. Two exceptions mentioned. The Rev. Edmund Wood of Montreal, and Dean Hellmuth, Archdeacon of Huron. Opinions on the Bishop of Huron's objections to the theological teaching in Trinity College, Toronto. The proceedings of the Provincial Synod. The Bishop of Rupert's Land. The Bishop of Toronto. Incidents attending the Metropolitan's death and funeral. Dean Bethune. Archdeacon Leach. Canon Bond. The 12th September, a marked anniversary in the annals of the Diocese of Montreal.

APPENDIX.

List of Persons who received Holy Orders from the Most Reverend Francis Fulford, D.D.

THE RIGHT REVEREND

GEORGE JEHOSHAPHAT MOUNTAIN, D.D., D.C.L.,

THIRD BISHOP OF QUEBEC.

CHAPTER ONE

The Mountain family of French descent. Huguenots. Louis the Fourteenth. Revocation of the Edict of Nantes. The policy of Richelieu and Mazarin carried out by Ann of Austria. Madame de Maintenon. Persecution of the Protestants. Their flight and their misfortunes. Consequences to the Gallican Church and to France. Disasters to French armies. The battle of Quebec and surrender of Canada. The Mountain family. The Huguenot immigrant, M. Jacob de Montaigne, a great grandson of the Essayist, Michel de Montaigne. His settlement in England. Marriage and death. Widow and two sons survive him. One of them, Jacob Mountain, educated at Cambridge. Enters Holy Orders. His marriage with Elizabeth Mildred Wale Kentish, of Little Bardfield Hall in the "Hundred of Dunmow." "The custom of Dunmow." How celebrated. Mr. Mountain's preferment to St. Andrews, Norwich. Selected by Dr. Tomlin, the Bishop of Lincoln, as his chaplain. Presented to the living of Buckden. Chosen as first Bishop of Quebec. George Jehoshaphat Mountain, the second son, born 27th July, 1789. Interesting historical coincidences. The Prince of Condé. Norwich rich in personal reminiscences. Archbishop Parker. Bishops Hall and Horne. Influence of their characters and work, on the future Bishop of Quebec. The difficulties of biographical narrative. Illustrated. The Rev. Armine W. Mountain's memoir of his father, an example. The Georgian Eras, an era of misfortune to the Anglican Church in North America and "the Indies." Their wretched ecclesiastical condition. Bishop Seabury. The Bishoprics of Nova Scotia and Quebec. The voyage of "the thirteen Mountains" from England to Canada. Their arrival at Quebec. The Gallican Bishop makes the Anglican Bishop welcome with a "kiss on both cheeks." Several reasons for such a fraternal welcome.

CHAPTER TWO

Woodfield in the vicinity of the city taken as the residence of the first Anglican Bishop of Quebec. Boyhood of his sons passed there. "On 28th March, 1796, George began his Latin grammar." The happiness afforded to him by the Greek and Latin poets in

Table of Contents.

after life. George and his elder brother sent to England for Education. Graduated at Trinity College, Cambridge. Recommended by Dr. Monk, Bishop of Gloucester, as Principal of a College in Nova Scotia. Returns to Quebec. Enters Holy Orders. Accompanies the Bishop on his triennial visitation. At the time of the visitation, four out of the seven Clergymen of the Anglican Church in Lower Canada bore the name of Mountain. Admitted to Priest's orders. Marries. Appointed Rector of Fredericton. Chaplain of the Garrison there, and also Chaplain of the Legislative Council of New Brunswick. Journey to Fredericton and how performed. Returns to Quebec. Appointed "Bishop's Official," Rector, and Archdeacon in 1821. Clerical career, how commenced and continued. Receives his degree of D.D. from Archbishop of Canterbury. Accompanies the Bishop on his last visitation. Stay at Cornwall. Anecdote. Meets with Hon. and Rev. C. J. Stewart, D.D. His character. Their friendship. Clergy Reserve question. Delegation to England thereon. Dr. Mountain always disinclined to struggle for temporalities. Disliked diplomacy and Parliamentary work. His only wish to preach the gospel. McGill College and Dr. Mountain's connection therewith. Reflection thereon. Again sent to England to negotiate on the subjects of the Clergy Reserves and the division of the Diocese. Ill success of his mission. Death of the Bishop, his father, unattended by any of his sons. Dr. Mountain returns to Canada. His touching reference to his mother. Dr. Stewart succeeds to the Bishopric. Overworked and breaks down. Dr. Mountain appointed Coadjutor. Death of Bishop Stewart. Dr. Mountain consecrated as the third Bishop of the undivided Diocese of Canada.

CHAPTER THREE.

The Diocese of Quebec. Its territorial extent. Dr. Mountain a missionary Bishop. His thoughts on the Church as a divine organization. Many of his opinions in accord with, but in advance of the "Oxford movement." The short comings of the Anglican church, illustrated. The satire of Macaulay. Consequences of the insular policy of English Churchmen. A change in such policy. Meeting at Willis' Rooms to extend the Episcopate in the Colonies. Effects of that meeting. Contrast between "now" and "then." Synodical action, a consequence of the increase in the Episcopate. Diocesan Synods. Provincial Synods. Dr. Mountain's exertions to obtain both. His advice sought with respect to the selection of a Metropolitan. Recommends that Montreal be the seat of the See, and Dr. Fulford the Metropolitan. Reasons therefor. Protests against an itinerant Primate. Montreal apparently ill suited to the reception and preservation of Royal favours. Illustrations of local caprice. Some reflections on the appointment of Metropolitan. Earlier work of Dr. Mountain. Parish institutions, Schools, Asylums, Societies, established by him. Ministerial work on Sundays and week days. Heroic charity during cholera season of 1832-4. Appalling statistics. Again in the ship fever season of 1847. Bravely supported by his clergy. Names of those who took duty with him at Grosse Isle. Statistics. Reflections. Requested by the Church Missionary Society to visit the Red River Territories. His visit. A Bishopric established there. *Songs of the Wilderness* written then. The Bishopric of Sierra Leone and his intentions with respect to it. How the Bishop was hindered and opposed, and by whom. His generosity and forbearance of character. His patience and gentleness. Anecdotes illustrative thereof. The remark that the Bishop "was but an indifferent administrator" not well founded, and why. Neither a sectarian nor a political Bishop. Dean Goodwin's description of Bishop MacKenzie, strictly applicable to Bishop Mountain. A Jubilee service on the completion of the fiftieth year of his ministry. How celebrated. "The Mountain Jubilee scholarship" founded. The end approaches. The year of release follows the year of Jubilee. Great peacefulness in his Diocese. Apparent renewal of bodily strength. Hardship and exposure. A mission established and a missionary sent to Labrador. Advent solemnities. Christmas joys. The Bishop's sermon on Christmas day. His absence from church on the following Holy-days. Anxiety thereat. The closing scene. His children and grand children kneel and receive his blessing. His last words. His death on the Festival of the Epiphany. The Funeral.

APPENDIX.

List of persons admitted to Holy Orders by the Right Rev. GEORGE JEHOSHAPHAT MOUNTAIN, D.D., D.C.L., the Third Bishop of Quebec.

THE HON. AND RIGHT. REV.

JOHN STRACHAN, D.D., LL.D.,

FIRST BISHOP OF TORONTO.

CHAPTER ONE.

Similar traits in the character of Lord Chancellor Eldon and the first Bishop of Toronto. They "never ratted." Popular opinion of the latter. The Bishop's account of his parentage and education. His father a *non juror*, his mother a member of the Relief denomination. The early death of the former and the absolute influence of the latter. The Bishop's reverence for his mother's memory. His strong religious feelings. His unsettled theological opinions. Had by no religious act of his own attached himself to any Christian denomination. Episcopacy in Scotland at the time of his birth. The period an important one in the history of America. The independence of the thirteen rebellious provinces. The North American Loyalists. Their partial settlement in Canada. They were the Bishop's earliest friends in Canada. Their principles gave direction to his opinions. His previous history. Birth at Kettle. Education at King's College, Aberdeen. Obtains his degree. After a severe competition appointed master of the Parish School of Kettle, when only nineteen years of age. That competition the turning point in his life. His Aberdeen accent. His indomitable will. His youthful aspect. Consequent hesitancy of the elders to give him the appointment of schoolmaster. How they were influenced. His pupils at Kettle, Sir David Wilkie, Commodore Barclay. Removes to the Glasgow University. The retirement of his patron, the Rev. Professor Brown. His great disappointment thereat. Affairs in Canada. The settlement of the U. E. Loyalists therein. Their character and sacrifices. The appreciation of both by the King and people of England. Upper Canada erected into a separate Province. Governor Simcoe. His opening speech at Niagara. The creation of the Bishopric of Quebec. The Right Reverend Jacob Mountain, Bishop of Quebec. Called to the Executive Council of Upper Canada. The probable reason for such proceeding. The Constitution to be made symmetrical in Church and State. Reflections thereon. Governor Simcoe's desire to establish a University. The Bishop's account of the transaction. The office of Principal offered to Mr. Duncan and to Dr. Chalmers. Declined by them. Accepted by Dr. Strachan, who sails from Greenock. Arrives at Kingston,

Table of Contents. xv

U. C., on the last day of the year 1799. Learns that Governor Simcoe had returned to England. His disappointment thereat. How obliged to act. Accepts the situation of tutor to Mr. Cartwright's sons at Kingston. Meets Archdeacon Stuart, and after counsel and examination takes orders in the Anglican Church. Ordained by the Bishop of Quebec. That Prelate's impression of his character. Removes to the mission of Cornwall. Establishes the Cornwall school. Popular views of the "Church by law established," and the tendency of such views. Impressions of many Scotsmen thereupon. Effects of such views in Canada. Archdeacon Fuller describes the Bishop's impressions of his life at Cornwall. His marriage there. University honours conferred on him. Appointed Rector of York. The influence of the Cornwall scholars The oldest surviving "boy" supposed to be Dean Bethune of Montreal. The Bishop's residence at Cornwall and what he did there. The war of 1812. The Bishop removed from Cornwall at the instance of Major-General Sir Isaac Brock. Appointed Rector of York. Probable reasons therefor. The Bishop's pluck and resolution. An example thereof, on his passage from Kingston to Toronto.

Chapter Two.

The Rector of York, arrives at York (now Toronto). Lays himself out for work. The war of 1812. Establishes "the Loyal and Patriotic Society." The battle of York. "The little Rector" combines several characters in his own person. Priest, soldier, and diplomatist. Encounter with a "looting" party of American soldiers at Colonel Givens' house. The firmness of "the little Rector." Dramatic situation. The result. Appointed by the authorities to negotiate with General Dearborn. A stirring altercation. The General's menace answered with a clergyman's threat. The result. The Bishop's successful services in seasons of peril inclined people to regard him with favour in seasons of peace. The war ended. The Bishop regarded as a wise councillor. His influence. The exercise of power begets a love of power. His clerical office regarded by many as a qualification for secular duty. The reason why. The difficulty of combining the spiritual and temporal orders in the same ruler. The Bishop intends to serve the Church by accepting service in the State. Wishes to assimilate the constitution of Upper Canada to that of the United Kingdom. Plausible reasons for his opinions. The Union of church and state. Advantages thereof. Upper Canada to be mapped out in parishes.

Each parish to be the resident centre of a clergyman of the national Church. Desire to consolidate the Protestant forces of Upper Canada, and to resist the encroachments of Rome. Such a policy successfully resisted by combinations of Protestants. The Bishop refused to give up. No difficulties deterred him. Example. His political principles not of a progressive type. Pays little attention to the current of public opinion, and holds in contempt politicians who like weathercocks seem always to be waiting for the wind. He was "as tenacious as a Scot." Matters of principle did not admit of conditions. Hence his struggle for "the truth, the whole truth and nothing but the truth." The Clergy Reserve question. How and by whom it was opened. Sir Peregrine Maitland and Earl Bathurst thereon. The petition of the Clergy Reserve corporation. How the question was managed and mismanaged. The result, defeat. The University question. The Bishop's labours thereon. Those labours in harmony with his opinions on the question "what is education." The Bishop's exertions end in defeat. Reflections thereon. The Church party and its opponents. Strong prejudices and conflicting principles. Is the University question settled? Disappointment did not occasion despair. Discarding Royal gifts and Provincial charters, as of little value, the Bishop appeals to the voluntary principle, to honour and self-interest; to virtue and religion. The University of Trinity College, Toronto. The result of such appeal. That "child of his old age," his "joy of grief" his fittest monument, and the most touching expression of his faith: "I believe that God in all things should be glorified."

CHAPTER THREE.

The Right Hon. W. E. Gladstone on *The State and its relations with the Church*. The Right Reverend John Strachan consecrated First Bishop of Toronto. Discussions in the Upper Canada Legislature on the reunion of the Provinces. The Bishop's opinions thereon. The signature "John Toronto" first seen in the Journals of the Legislative Council affixed to a Protest against such reunion of the Provinces. The same signature last seen on the Journals affixed to a Protest against the secularization of the Clergy Reserves. Time had not shaken the Bishop's opinions or softened his phraseology Examples In sea phrase the Bishop was determined to go down with his flags flying He did so His letter, fifteen years later, on the same subject to the Hon. A. N. Morin, is all aglow with heat and anger, with reproach and menace. Reflections on the style in which theologians too commonly discuss the charities of religion. Some excuse for the Bishop since it is not easy to suffer and be kind. All the objects for which he had striven as a politician seemed to perish or to elude him. Almost all the measures he opposed as a churchman, have been carried by churchmen who have succeeded him. The Clergy Reserve, the University, and the Common School questions represent successive defeats. The Bishop cherished most of the aversions of a Tory, and he had none of the softness of a Whig. He had a Johnsonian distrust of Non-conformists, and greatly desired that his Presbyterian friends would "purge themselves of the heresy of John Knox." He liked the theory of "a Church by law established," for he appreciated the privileges which such a theory included. Reflections thereon. Ecclesiastics who had discharged the duties of statesmen probably became subjects of the Bishop's study. Necessity of attaching supporters to his views. The means resorted to and the disadvantages that followed. Would a different course of procedure have resulted differently? Reasons for believing that a happier result would have followed from a less heated controversy. The Bishop's intercourse with his clergy characterized by kindness, generally supported them in disputes with their parishioners. He rebuked sharply. "Sit down, sir, you are talking nonsense." The Rev. Dr. Scadding's compliments on the "North British depth and breadth of the Bishop's 'deep chested music.'" Even "Rhaetian tones" did not make a rough manner pleasant. The Bishop's occasional style would be termed in England "Transatlantic." The Bishop recognized great latitude of opinion in his dealings with his clergy. He neither required an Islington password nor a Liturgical Shibboleth from clergymen who desired to work in his Diocese. Moral goodness lies at the root of all religion. An anecdote. The parish church rebuilt four times during the Bishop's residence at Toronto. He founded two Universities and one College. Originated the Church Society. Co-operated in the establishment of Cemeteries. Held the first Diocesan Synod in Canada. Concurred in the Canon for the creation of a Metropolitan See, and for holding Provincial Synods, and he initiated the sustentation fund for the support of his Clergy. The Bishop a voluminous writer, and a generous antagonist. His benevolence a proverb. He cared little for money, saved nothing and died poor. His sense of duty equalled by his courage. Both conspicuously exhibited in the cholera seasons of 1832-4. Religion less a sentiment than a duty. Truth always attracted him. He loved children. Time laid his hand upon him. He desired relief and assistance in the discharge of his duties. The Synod elect Archdeacon Bethune coadjutor. The Bishop dies on All Saints' Day of the same year. His appreciation of all legitimate aids to a holy life. Reflections with respect to the Bishop's observance

Table of Contents.

of the appointed holydays of the Church. Canon Dixon's reference to the last sermon the Bishop preached. It was seemly that the Festival of "All Saints" should have been the day appointed for him to pass through the grave and gate of death. Quotation from Keble. The Rev. Dr. Ryerson's notice of the Bishop's death. The funeral. Old pupils his pall-bearers. Imposing solemnities. Affecting service. Canon Baldwin. Dean Grasett. Canon Bevan. The place of interment in front of the holy table, hard by the place where on Sundays and holydays the Apostolic Benediction fell from his lips:

"The peace of God which passeth all understanding."

APPENDIX NO. 1.

Alphabetical List of " Young Gentlemen" now living, (i. e. 26th November, 1827)" who have been educated by the Honourable and Right Reverend John Strachan, D. D., Archdeacon of York (now Toronto) in Upper Canada.

The list in question is in the possession of Mr. Solomon Chesley of Ottawa, one of the Cornwall School " boys," and it has evidently been revised and corrected by the Bishop.

APPENDIX NO 2.

Trinity College, Toronto.—List of Professors ; also of Students who have matriculated at the University of Trinity College, Toronto, since its opening, together with other information relating thereto.

APPENDIX NO. 3.

Names of persons admitted to Holy Orders by the Honourable and Right Reverend JOHN STRACHAN, D.D., LL.D., First Bishop of Toronto.

Collect for Unity.

O God, the Father of our Lord Jesus Christ, our only Saviour, the Prince of Peace; Give us grace seriously to lay to heart the great dangers we are in by our unhappy divisions. Take away all hatred and prejudice, and whatsoever else may hinder us from godly Union and Concord: that, as there is but one Body and one Spirit, and one Hope of our Calling, one Lord, one Faith, one Baptism, one God and Father of us all, so we may henceforth be all of one heart, and of one soul, united in one holy bond of Truth and Peace, of Faith and Charity, and may with one mind and one mouth glorify Thee; through Jesus Christ our Lord. Amen.

The Most Reverend
Francis Fulford, D.D.,

Lord Bishop of Montreal and Metropolitan of Canada.

THE MOST REVEREND

FRANCIS FULFORD, D.D.,

LORD BISHOP OF MONTREAL,

AND

METROPOLITAN OF CANADA.

CHAPTER FIRST.

> True is, that whilome that good poet said
> That gentle mind by gentle deed is known;
> For man by nothing is so well bewray'd
> As by his manners, in which plain is shown
> Of what degree and what race he is grown.
> SPENSER'S *Faerie Queene*.

AT what particular period the adventurous ancestor of the Fulford family emerged from the forests of Germany, and established himself in the kingdom of Wessex, is not noted in the Herald's Chronicle; for Burke, in his history of the Landed Gentry, is content to begin the record of the race in the reign of Richard the First. From that authentic history we learn that the family is not only of Saxon origin, but that it was one of consideration and influence in the time of the Lion-hearted King.

"Folefort," as the place is written in Domesday Book, has been held by uninterrupted descent and with true West of England tenacity by the Fulford family for more than six hundred years. The estate, which is now in the possession of Colonel Fulford, the elder brother of the late Metropolitan, is in the parish of Dunsford and about nine miles south west of Exeter. The mansion, which is one of the oldest in the county, presents an imposing appearance, for it is built in a quadrangular form on an elevated plateau, and the enclosed grounds, which are thickly wooded, include an extensive and picturesque sheet of water. Over the entrance of the main gateway are the family arms quartering those of Fitz-Wise, Mereton, Belston, Bozom, St. George, Dennis, St. Aubyn and Shallons. In the days of the Plantagenets, perhaps under the pressure of the fashion introduced with the Normans, the old Saxon name of the place was changed to Villa-de-Fulford, but, with the subsidence of French influence, it was subsequently altered to the English name of Great Fulford, which it now bears. The apartments are numerous as well as spacious, and contain several fine and some curious paintings. Among the former is a full length portrait of Charles the First in his robes, by Vandyke. This picture was given to Sir Francis Fulford by the "Royal Martyr." Nor was the gift unworthily bestowed, for Sir Francis not only garrisoned his mansion for the King, but he lost it too, as it was taken in 1645 by a detachment of Fairfax's army. A private chapel was attached to the house, which, we believe, is still preserved. It is scarcely necessary to add that the family is one of the old historical county families, which are the pride and strength of the people of England. Though un-ennobled, such families enjoy the more ancient dignity, as they belong to the earlier degree of gentleman. Many knights of Great Fulford distinguished themselves at and after the time of the Crusades. They were also especially conspicuous during the Wars of the Roses, as well as for the King against Cromwell. One of them, Sir Thomas Fulford, accompanied " Lord Edward Courtenie, Earl of Devonshire, and the valiant Lord William, his sonne," and other knights and gentlemen of Devon on the expedition which successfully relieved Exeter when it was besieged by Perkin Warbeck, in 1497. Probably the Earl of Devon above mentioned was the Lord Edward, the good " Erle " whose memory, with that of Catherine his Countess, is sacredly preserved in St. Peter's Church, Tiverton. The inscription on the monument is amusingly quaint, and though somewhat beside our subject, is not unworthy of a place among Devonshire reminiscences:

> " Hoe! hoe! who lies here?
> 'Tis I, the good Erle of Devonshire,
> With Kate my wife, to mee full deer;
> We lived together fyfte-fyve yeere.
> That wee spent, wee had,
> That wee lefte, wee loste,
> That wee gave, we have!"

Gallantry, too, seems to have been as conspicuous as courage, for Prince, in his *Worthies of Devon*, quaintly narrates that Sir Baldwin de Fulford " was a great soldier, and a traveller of so undaunted a resolution, that for the honour and liberty of a royal lady, in a castle besieged by the infidels, he fought a combat with a Saracen, for bulk and bigness an unequal match (as the representation of him cut in the wainscot in Fulford Hall doth plainly show,) whom yet he vanquished, and rescued the lady." The old chronicle does not inform us in what language whether of pantomime or of speech, the gallant knight and royal lady exchanged compliments, or expressed obligations. The wainscot of Great Fulford whispers no secrets, and the portrait tells no tales; neither is the guerdon which the rescued captive may be supposed to have bestowed upon her deliverer, found among the transmitted curiosities of the race. Such an adventure ought to have had a fitting termination. Poetry and moonlight should have blended their influences and have shed something more than a passing sentiment on the scene; for the Knight and the Lady should "have lived happily together ever afterwards." As lovers of romance, we hope that they did so, but, as faithful historians, we are obliged to add that no register of the fact has come under our notice.

Besides the quality of audacity which attached to the martial members of the race, the quality of indifference, which sometimes is akin to courage, was conspicuous in at least one of the legal representatives of the family. In the year 1403, for example, the celebrated Chief Justice Sir William Gascoigne, and the less famous Sir William Fulford, who, we assume, must have been a Puisné Judge, appear to have been associated with the Earl of Westmoreland in a commission for levying forces against the insurrection of Henry Percy, the celebrated Hotspur. Two years afterwards, on the apprehension of Scroope, Archbishop of York, the Chief Justice refused, even at the command of the King, to sentence that prelate to death as a traitor, because, as he alleged, the law gave him no jurisdiction over the life of an ecclesiastic. Sir William Fulford apparently read the law differently, or it may have been, he either was a less scrupulous minister of justice, or that he held opinions more severe and decided on the superior advantages of summary punishment. At all events his conscience was less harassed with legal technicalities. Like other members of his house, he wore the red rose in his heart as well as on his breast, and, perchance, the reflection of that sanguinary flower may have coloured his feelings and inflamed his judgment; for having the gratification of the King rather than the fear of the Pope before his eyes, he no more hesitated to pass sentence of death on the Archbishop, than did Henry the Fourth to let the sentence take effect. Like the Courtneys, Earls of Devon, the Fulfords seem to have been ardent Lancastrians, and, like them, to have contributed a few lives to the cause they espoused. In 1461, at the memorable battle of Towton Field, so disastrous to the fortunes of the red rose, Sir Thomas, a son of Sir Baldwin Fulford, commanded a division of Queen Margaret's army, and being taken prisoner by the Yorkists, the farce of a trial and the fact of an execution speedily followed. He, like many others, was beheaded.

Passing over the remote, and we may add the romantic portion of the family history, and coming down to the present century, we may observe that the late Metropolitan was the second son of Baldwin Fulford, Esq., of Great Fulford, and that he was born at Sidmouth on the 3rd of June, 1803. Having received his earlier education at Tiverton, he entered Exeter College, Oxford, in 1821. In 1824 he won his B.A. degree, and in the following year was elected a Fellow of his college. In 1826 he was ordained Deacon, at Norwich Cathedral, and Priest on the 22nd of June, 1828, in the Cathedral of Exeter. In 1830, he married Mary, eldest daughter of Andrew Berkeley Drummond, Esq., of Cadland, Hants, and the Lady Mary, his wife, a daughter of John, second Earl of Egmont, and sister of the Right Honourable Spencer Percival, who, while holding the office of First Lord of the Treasury, and being at the same time Prime Minister of England, was murdered by Bellingham in the lobby of the House of Commons.

After filling successive curacies in two parishes, the late Metropolitan was instituted by the Duke of Rutland, the patron of the living, to the Rectory of Trowbridge, in Wiltshire, a town with a large manufacturing population and a spacious church. In this town he resided from 1832 to 1842. To his clerical experiences he there added a practical acquaintance with judicial duties, for, from the dearth of persons resident, qualified to serve in the Commission of the Peace, he acted, at the request of the government, for several years as a Magistrate, and from what was subsequently seen of his aptitude and capacity, there can be little doubt that as a judge, as well as a clergyman, he commanded respect and conciliated good will. In 1838 he received his M.A. degree, and was appointed Chaplain to Her Royal Highness the late Duchess of Gloucester. In 1842 he resigned the Rectory of Trowbridge, and accepted the Rectory of Croydon, in Cambridgeshire, which he held until 1845, when, on the nomination of Earl Howe, he was licensed by the late Bishop of London as minister of Curzon Chapel, Mayfair. This appointment he held until his selection by Her Majesty as the first Bishop of the new Diocese of Montreal. The honorary degree of D.D. was then conferred on him by the University of Oxford, and he was consecrated at Westminster Abbey on the 25th of July, 1850, being the Festival of St. James the Apostle.

And here the reflection will probably occur to many, and especially to those who are acquainted with English localities, as well as with clerical duties in England, that the varied experiences of ministerial life which the Bishop acquired were valuable introductions to his later and more exalted positions. His first curacy, for instance, at Holne, in Dartmoor, from the isolated character of its surroundings, in some respects resembled the backwoods of Canada. Fawley, his second curacy, like some of the older livings of the Dominion, was situated in a rich and picturesque agricultural county. His institution as Rector of Trowbridge placed him in the midst of a large manufacturing population, where much prejudice had to be met, and many forms of dissent to be dealt with, while his knowledge acquired there as a magistrate made him familiar with some of the rules which are supposed to govern those who are called upon to analyze evidence or to administer justice. Curzon Chapel, Mayfair, seated in the aristocratic quarter of the Metropolis, would naturally attract a highly educated congregation. Doubtless, such experiences exerted a powerful influence on his mind, and were of great service to him in later life. Nor was his work in England unmarked by the people whom he served. Evidences of popular affection and esteem remain, as sacred heirlooms in his family, to attest that, however versatile his talents, and however varied his experience, there was one kind of service which equally attracted different interests, and secured the affection of different classes, while it won from all spontaneous expressions of good will. Thus, the manufacturers and artizans of Trowbridge, and the nobility and gentry of Mayfair, were moved by kindred sentiments when they sought by imperishable gifts to be remembered kindly by the friend and clergyman on whom those gifts were bestowed. The former presented him with a tea service of silver, and the latter with an antique grace cup of the like precious substance, accompanied with three hundred and sixty sovereigns.

Not only was the Bishop a hard-working parish priest, but he did good service in the literary forces of the Church. When the *Colonial Church Chronicle* was first started, he was chosen as its trusted editor, and in this way acquired a very intimate, as well as extensive acquaintance with the condition and resources of the Colonial Church. Again, while Rector of Trowbridge, he found time to publish two volumes of *Plain Sermons on the Church and her Services*, as well as a short treatise on the *Progress of the Reformation in England*.

Turning from England to Canada, from the newly consecrated Bishop to the newly constituted Diocese, certain facts present themselves which should not be overlooked. In 1793, the Right Reverend Jacob Mountain, D.D., was consecrated as the first Bishop of Quebec, a diocese literally representing a "boundless contiguity of shade," whose limits were, at least, co-extensive with the Provinces of Upper and Lower Canada. After laboring for twenty-five years, that Prelate petitioned for a division of his See, offering to relinquish £1000 per annum of his stipend towards the support of a bishop for the Western Province. To accomplish this holy purpose, he sent his son, the Reverend George Jehoshaphat Mountain, to England, to make the necessary representations to, and arrangements with, the authorities; but that earnest and self-denying clergyman returned without accomplishing the object of his mission. The holy aim of the Bishop's later days was not to be gratified in his time, for having presided over the Canadian diocese for thirty-two years, he departed this life, and was succeeded by the Honourable and Right Reverend Charles J. Stewart, D.D. That estimable prelate sought to accomplish what his predecessor had vainly striven to obtain; but his efforts were but partially successful. The authorities would not consent to a division of the diocese, but they agreed to the minor proposition, and associated the Right Reverend George Jehoshaphat Mountain with him as Suffragan, with the title of Bishop of Montreal. On the death of Bishop Stewart, the latter became his successor in the See of Quebec, but nevertheless he retained the title under which he had been consecrated, sagaciously observing as his reason for doing so, that it was advisable to familiarize the people of England, as well as the people of Canada with the title of Bishop of Montreal, as it might, and perhaps would, suggest to both the necessity for creating a diocese to correspond with the title. At length, after a period of forty-six years, and after many earnest petitions had been presented therefor, the British Government authorized the division of the Diocese of Quebec, which thenceforward, for ecclesiastical purposes, was to be separated into Upper and Lower Canada, the former section representing the Diocese of Toronto, and the latter the Diocese of Quebec. Distant as the prospect then seemed of a further subdivision of the latter diocese, the Bishop of Quebec would not part with the hope, and therefore he still continued to subscribe himself by the title of Bishop of Montreal ; for being full of faith and abounding in zeal, he religiously looked forward to the day when that subscription by whomsoever made, would represent something more than a name.

But while hope was deferred in Canada, and "the watchmen" at different intervals inquired wearily of one another, "what of the night," an extraordinary awakening of Church thought and Church feeling was going on in the most ancient seats of Church learning in the mother country. Though by no means deficient in poetic attraction, the new movement sprang almost entirely from an intellectual root. It laid the mind and the judgment under tribute, since it appealed directly to history and to reason, and only incidentally to sentiment and to tradition. The public conscience was sensibly smitten, for the astute clergymen of Oxford who made the pulpit and the press their ministers, took especial pains to compare religion as it was, with religion as it had been and as it should be. The exposition electrified the age, and a thrill of devout thought was sent from land to land; from the seat of Empire to the most distant possession of the British Crown. The springs of charity and benevolence were touched to the quick, and the souls thus inspirited sought in sacrifice and alms deeds, in culture and study, in daily prayer and frequent communion for fitting expressions of their faith as well as of their enthusiasm. The zeal awakened by such means, and under such circumstances, was necessarily more moral than political, more catholic than sectarian, more expanding than selfish, and thus it was that those earnest Oxford voices, which first fell on the bright waters of the Isis, were wafted across every sea, to find an echo on every shore where the British flag is seen, or the English language is spoken.

When referring to that movement, in its relation to the religious transactions of the sixteenth century, it may be as well to bear in mind that the late Metropolitan had very thoughtfully studied the characters of the Reformers when he penned his history of the Reformation. His love for catholic truth gave force to his reverence for those who, in the defence of that truth, had protested against foreign usurpation and dangerous errors. We, therefore, may well imagine the intense scorn with which he must, in recent days, have regarded their degeneracy, who, claiming to be the successors of the great men, his Oxford contemporaries, as well as ordained ministers of the Anglican Church, had, nevertheless so degraded themselves as to speak abominable things of the confessors and martyrs of that church:—who with ribald tongues had defamed their memories, and with unclean lips had spat upon their tombs. Verily, and of a truth, such persons defile the white vestments which the law allows them to wear, and shame the order whose sanctity they are bound to uphold. Neither are their sentiments the legitimate offspring of Oxford thought, as it found expression thirty-five years ago—of that earnest thought whose influence reached the intellect of Catholic as well as of Protestant Christendom, and is still apparent far beyond the limits of the Anglican Church. The impression of that thought is at this day everywhere conspicuous. It may be seen in the plans and contrivances of different religious bodies for a closer and more intimate fellowship. It may be heard in the supplications of almost every Christian association for greater union among Christian people. It may be observed in the use of forms of prayer and of liturgical offices, where forms of prayer and liturgical offices were never before used. It may be heard in the service of praise, where with respect to instrumental music, the ban is removed and the forbidden breath of the organ, for the first time, is blended with the breath of humanity in ascribing glory, and honor, and praise to God. It is visible in the architecture of places built for holy worship, where in matters of external beauty and of internal arrangement, even the puritan mind rejects the prejudice of Knox, that it may do homage to the wisdom of Solomon.

The gifted men, who originated that great moral and religious movement, were in most cases the contemporaries at Oxford of the future Metropolitan of Canada. Some, it is true, like Demas of old, "have forsaken us," or like Ephraim, are "joined to their idols;" but for the most part they live for or have died in the Church whose faith they professed. They were men of rare gifts and original powers, who touched as with a live coal the religious life of the nation, awoke its dormant intellect, and, God helping them, turned both into channels of usefulness. They became the media through which the voices of past ages spoke to the present generation, and by which much of the mental wealth of antiquity was made available to contemporary times. Without mentioning masters and professors, whose careers have constantly been before the public for the last thirty-five years, we might note many familiar missionary names of lesser fame in the world of letters, but it may be of equal brightness in the "book of life." For example, the name of Ernest Hawkins will be found in the Oxford Book, in the honour class of 1824, not far above the name of Francis Fulford. The late Bishop of Rupert's Land was a member of the same College, while Dr. Field, the present Bishop of Newfoundland, and Dr. Medley, the present Bishop of Fredericton, were contemporary undergraduates of the same university. And with respect to the Reverend Canon Hawkins, it may be noted that he not only succeeded the Reverend Francis Fulford as the incumbent of Curzon Chapel, Mayfair, but that in the procession of mortality he followed him closely to the grave, for, if we mistake not, the former departed this life three weeks after the latter had entered into rest. The name of Ernest Hawkins will always be cherished with affectionate regard by the members of the Anglican Church in the Colonies. For the space of a quarter of a century he was the indefatigable Secretary of the Society for the Propagation of the Gospel in Foreign parts, and from its formation in 1841, it was his privilege to be the honorary and hard-working Secretary of the Society for the establishment of Colonial Bishoprics.

The organization of the Anglican Church in the Colonies was among the earliest of the numerous benefits which followed and perhaps helped to bring about the Oxford movement. The late Bishop of Quebec had inherited the hopes of his predecessors in the See, and had given them consistency by doing what lay in his power to secure for Canada an early portion of that benefit. Plans had been made and were already ripening under his observation for a further division of his diocese and for the permanent endowment of a new one. Those who knew that venerable Prelate can best testify with what boundless gratitude his heart burned within him when the news arrived that Her Majesty had been graciously pleased to acquiesce in such plans, and by Letters Patent had not only set apart a new diocese in Canada, under the name of the Diocese of Montreal, but had appointed the Right Reverend Francis Fulford, D.D., to be the first Bishop.

Nevertheless, the season was one of great religious excitement in Canada. The Oxford movement had sensibly advanced, and the fruits of that movement had become the subject of much alarm in some, and of very serious discussion in many quarters. Its progress awed the timid and made the bold pause, for it seemed to have reached a point where perils threatened, and anxiety was felt. Nor should it be overlooked that the great religious questions of the day were, and perhaps are as warmly, if not as argumentatively, discussed in Canada as in England, for the inhabitants of the Colonies claim their inheritance in the thought as well as in the blood of the mother country. "The Hampden Scandal," as it was termed by some, had excited profound attention; while "The Gorham Controversy" was sufficiently distressing to disquiet the discussions of all. The presence of a Bishop resident at Montreal was especially desirable, for the notes of controversy, the cry of alarm, which then disheartened the Church in England, had been borne across the Atlantic to the discomfort of the Church in Canada. Good people with more feeling than reason, and whose knowledge was scarcely equal to their zeal, appeared to think that the peace of the Church here could best be promoted by an effort to naturalize the cries that were disturbing the Church at home, and thus it happened that the Protestants of Montreal found themselves whirled about in a flurry of phrases, whose meanings were generally the reflections of the coteries that used them, rather than of the facts they were supposed to interpret. Hence it happened that, with little knowledge and less consideration, people suddenly determined their party principles irrespective of the grounds for such determination. A good deal of clerical passion, and a good deal of lay prejudice were abroad, the former finding its escape in the pulpit, and the latter in the press; one party denounced and the other threatened. Both excited the feelings, but neither satisfied the judgment, and thus the difficulty became almost as great to silence a cry which had sprung from no adequate cause, as it was to discover the cause of the cry. The missionary work of the Missionary Church of Canada was disturbed and hindered by questions which people asked with ease, but answered with difficulty, for men's minds were misty as well as heated. Disputants affirmed with less labour than they investigated, and as it was more convenient to say sharp things than wise ones, some found a solace in escaping from the inconvenience of the latter that they might practice the irresponsibility of the former. Others again discovered that it was more easy to determine a colour than to unravel a controversy, and therefore ecclesiastical vestments became so to speak the badges of the opposing parties; and such mysterious subjects as the manner of a sinner's justification, of sacramental grace, of Divine decrees and of human accountability, seemed in some indistinct way, to be associated with, if not explained by, the accident of a clergyman preaching in a surplice or a gown.

Quiet Churchmen, who were accustomed to think that the path of religion like the path of virtue, should be one of pleasantness as well as of peace, were ill able to be patient with respect to questions that seemed so trivial, and were so disturbing. Therefore the lovers of peace had especial reason to be thankful when a chief ruler of the new diocese was appointed, who, to "the fear of the Lord which is the beginning of wisdom," might be expected to "exercise a right judgment in all things." At all events, they were comforted by knowing that the Royal choice had fallen on a clergyman who had been educated in the most ancient seat of theological learning; who had gathered knowledge in the wide English field of parochial observation; who might be expected to impart counsel as one having experience, and to give judgment as one having authority; who could know nothing of our littleness and was a stranger to our strifes; who had no local enmities to appease, and no local friendships to reward, and who would be recognized as a fair representative of the piety and charity as well as of the genius and character of the Anglican Church. In the administration of her affairs such an one might be expected to blend gentleness and dignity with generosity of sentiment and liberality of thought; to settle our controversies with wisdom and not with temper, and to shame our enmities with courtesy and not with scorn. In short, the virtues and goodness of such an one would, it was fervently believed, so shine before men, as to constrain all who should take knowledge of him, to say with the first Christians under similiar circumstances, "that he had been with Jesus."

Chapter Second.

Give not thy tongue too great liberty, lest it take thee prisoner. A word unspoken is like a sword in the scabbard, thine. If vented, thy sword is in another's hand. If thou desire to be held wise, be so wise as to hold thy tongue.

QUARLES.

WHEN the first Anglican Bishop arrived at Quebec, he was courteously welcomed by the Gallican Bishop, who, with a kiss on both cheeks, expressed the pleasure he felt in receiving his episcopal brother, for, continued the Canadian prelate, "your people want you very badly." The commentary of a keen observer, at the close of the last century, might have been repeated with equal truth in the middle of the present century; for, certainly, those who can remember the disquieted state of the church population of Montreal at that time, will probably agree in thinking that the Bishop did not arrive at all too soon, and that his people "wanted him very badly."

The clergy and laity, though for different reasons, were naturally anxious to find out what manner of man their new Bishop was; and the former were especially curious to distinguish, if they could, the lights and shades of his theological character, to the end they might ascertain whether according to the canons of popular criticism, he was "high," "dry," "low," or "broad" church. But the subject of such irrepressible interest was strongly and on principle averse to gratify mere idle curiosity; more especially as it was his solemn resolve to become neither the lion of a sect, nor the leader of a party. Not that he was accustomed to conceal his opinions when a fitting occasion for expressing those opinions arose, but he did not deem it to be his duty to play the part of a garrulous prelate, and speak out of season because some egotistical presbyters unseasonably prompted him to do so. The Arab proverb: "Speech is silver, but silence is gold," was as well known to, as it was wisely practised by him, for his passages of silence were quite as useful, and sometimes more intelligible, than the maze of words through which mere chatterers commonly drag their ideas. "There is a time for silence," wrote the wise man, and few persons better than the Bishop understood when to determine that time. Nevertheless, such governing qualities as he pre-eminently possessed, had not been appreciated, much less practised by the people over whom he had been appointed to rule. The value of silence, for example, is but slightly esteemed in young communities, whose members, for the most part, chafe and fret for opportunities of airing their opinions and of making themselves heard. People who are constitutionally, or from habit, disposed to be rash, usually misinterpret, or underrate, those who for any reason are inclined to be reserved. At the time we speak of, it mattered little whether the subjects were theological or political, the propensity to write and talk violently, "to speak out," to "define positions," and to "have one word more," was sufficiently apparent. Being outspoken, as well as disputatious, the English part of the community did not very well know what to make of one whose tastes and habits seemed in no wise to harmonize with theirs. Therefore it chanced that between the period of the Bishop's appointment and the time of his arrival in Canada, a good many letters of a speculative kind were sent across the Atlantic. The clergy were particularly anxious to know what he had written, and especially whether he had said anything on "the Hampden Scandal," or the "Gorham Controversy," or with respect to the "Surplice Question." The laity, in like manner, were beset with some reasonable cravings on other though scarcely less important subjects. They wished, for example, to learn if he were a large-minded as well as a right minded man, whose Christianity would not be narrowed and contracted after their microscopic manner, whose theology is as attenuated and obscure as is the calligraphy of the ingenious people who spend their days in writing the Lord's Prayer on a sixpence. Of course there were, for there generally are certain irascible politicians of the old church and state type, who were eager to know whether the Bishop was a tory, a whig, or a member of the new composite party which had just inherited the name with the principles of the late Sir Robert Peel. Reliable information was not absolutely available, but the impression gathered strength with time that the Bishop's opinions were subjects of which he alone was the master, and moreover that he would not discover their meaning until the time arrived when such discovery might be made with advantage. What appeared to be certain was exactly what was not satisfactory, for the Bishop seemed neither to be a partizan nor a politician, but an earnest-minded minister of the church, who had no intention whatever of presenting the Gospel in a mask, or of disclosing only one half of its true features. It was conjectured, from what had been learned of the influences that had brought about his appointment, that he was one who, by " his preaching and living," would show that he regarded the honour of the church and the work of the church as something apart from and superior to, any fanciful form of theological thought, or any particular attitude of ecclesiastical attention.

People were probably conjecturing thus on the 12th of September, 1850, when, as the *Montreal Gazette* narrates, " the Bishop of Montreal, accompanied by Mrs. Fulford and their son and daughter, arrived at half-past seven o'clock in the morning, in the steamer Burlington, at St. John's," where, as the careful chronicler informs us, his Lordship was met by the Bishop of Quebec, and a number of the clergy and laity of the diocese of Montreal. After divine service had been celebrated in the parish church of St. John's, and an address of congratulation presented by the clergy and churchwardens of the Richelieu District, the whole party did, what English people commonly do on all occasions of rejoicing, they " partook of a sumptuous luncheon," which, we may add, was hospitably provided by a prominent layman of the place. It was then, or at a similar entertainment given on another occasion, though it may have been somewhat later in his career, that the occurrence took place which, as a matter of fact and not of chronology, we introduce here. The curiosity of the clergy generally was conspicuous enough, but it assailed a small coterie resident in the District of Richelieu in the form of an epidemic, until it apparently became too insupportable to be repressed. The coterie was composed of earnest, well-meaning gentlemen, whose piety and devotedness commanded respect, and received consideration. But while those gentlemen were deservedly admired for their zeal, they were probably less considered for their learning, and scarcely trusted for their discretion. Their theology was minute and one sided, sad and cheerless in its aspect, and frigid and severe in its operation; thus, while their religious system was narrow, selfish and sectarian, it was justly regarded as too illiberal and imperious to be accounted a fair and true expression of the faith and practice of the Church of England. Of course those gentlemen very naturally, and according to their lights very consistently, thought otherwise, and hence they were overcome by an insatiable desire to discover whether their new Bishop agreed with them, or with those from whom they differed. After an interchange of anxieties, and a conference among themselves, the exceedingly uncomfortable duty of asking an awkward, not to say an unbecoming question, was either allotted to, or assumed by, one of their number, a very estimable, though, as we have heard, a somewhat egotistical member of the party. The banquet was over. The decanters, we may conjecture, had glided with more than usual leisure round the table, and had probably rested at the point of departure. The ladies, having sipped or avoided the one glass of wine that is usually allotted to them, had retired. The rustling of brocades, and the whispering of illusion had died on the ear, and the shimmering of silks had been shut out of sight, for the drawing room door was closed. A pause succeeded, and a very trying one, too, when the initiatory step, in accordance with previous arrangement, was taken by the adventurous clergyman, who, like Archie of Scottish story, had bound himself to "bell the cat." Taking the earliest advantage of a lull in the conversation, and perchance being at the last moment desirous of getting rid of a duty which we should suppose became less supportable with delay, the anxious catechist went bravely and without circumlocution to the point. Seating himself opposite to, and at the same time addressing the Bishop, he is reported to have said: "In the first place, my lord, I shall frankly make a confession with respect to myself, and then I shall as frankly ask a question with respect to your lordship." Now the Bishop was one of those calm Englishmen whom it was difficult to surprise and not easy to perplex. Those who knew him will easily recall his massive expression and imperturbable manner, his calm, earnest, untroubled eyes, with their steel and bronze tints. They will remember, too, the suppressed humour, the ill-concealed mirthfulness that lodged mischievously near his eyebrows, or lingered patiently in the lines of his mouth. Neither will they forget the courtly attitude of high bred attention which he habitually wore, but which he more pointedly assumed when any one addressed him. They will probably fill up for themselves the outline picture which we have attempted to give, and their own recollection of the original will enable them to supply the expression of curious amazement which his face must have worn for the occasion, as, without preface or circumlocution, he heard himself addressed by the excited rector somewhat in the following words: "I am a low churchman, my lord, a very low churchman I may say!" but before the declaration was supplemented with the threatened question, the Bishop broke the thread of inquiry by observing, in words of measured gravity: "By which I hope you mean, Mr. Blank, that you are a very humble churchman!" Then turning to his host after the manner of one who knew how to direct as well as how to rebuke, added : " I think we had better join the ladies." How Mr. Blank and his colleagues looked as they joined the ladies, the ladies may remember, and our readers must imagine.

On arriving at Montreal, the Bishop was warmly received by the clergy and laity, who presented separate addresses of welcome, wherein they expressed their hearty desire to co-operate earnestly and faithfully with him in his labours for the spread of the Gospel and the interests of the church of God. We shall insert in full the Bishop's answer to the address of the clergy, and add one or two extracts from his answer to the address of the laity, for the first, like the last official words of a good man, are generally interesting.

Dr. Bethune,

I receive, with sincere thanks, the kind welcome and hearty congratulations expressed in the Address which you have now presented to me in the name of the Clergy of the Diocese of Montreal, on this my first arrival. I esteem myself most fortunate in having been called to preside over a Diocese which has so long enjoyed the able superintendence of your late respected Diocesan, and in which I shall find so large a body of the clergy devoting themselves, as I have good reason for believing is the case, with zeal and single-heartedness, to the work of the ministry. I trust that the measure now completed, whereby you have been provided with a Bishop for the separate Diocese of Montreal, by enabling your Diocesan to be brought into more frequent communication with all his clergy, to make more regular visitations through the several parishes, and give more distinct and careful attention to the various details which may be brought under his notice, will be productive of all that benefit to the Church which we have been led to anticipate.

But when I contemplate the wide and arduous field of duty that is opened before me, and remember my own insufficiencies and weaknesses, I do, indeed, look with strong confidence and hope to your assurance of your hearty desire to co-operate earnestly and faithfully with me in my labours for the spread of the Gospel and the interests of the Church of God; and, above all, I rely upon your continuing to offer up constant prayers that I may be encouraged and strengthened by God's Holy Spirit in the discharge of my important duties.

I will only further observe, that it will be my earnest desire to take the earliest opportunity of becoming personally acquainted with all my clergy, and I hope to live amongst them in the closest relations of confidential intercourse and mutual regard.

Speaking to the late Mr. Gerrard, as representing the laity, the Bishop among other things said :—

The assurance you have given me of your cordial co-operation with me is a great encouragement to me at the commencement of my administration of the affairs of this extended Diocese. It will be to you, gentlemen, that I shall look with hope and confidence. I feel that, coming amongst you as a stranger, I shall have much to learn before I shall be fully acquainted with all the details of your social condition, your habits of life and thought, the actual state of my Diocese, its wants, and the best advised and most practicable ways of supplying them. I rely upon your bearing with me while I am endeavouring to identify myself with you in all the relations of life, that you will give me credit for an anxious desire to do that which is right and just, and support me in the discharge of my arduous duties. And if we be not wanting to ourselves, I confidently anticipate that the increasing life and energy which always accompany the full development of Divine institutions, will be so manifested amongst us, that the Church will be enabled, year by year, to occupy a more fixed and substantive position, one more commensurate with the requirements of so large and useful a Diocese.

Certainly we cannot in any more fitting way do our duty to God and evince our gratitude for the munificence of those friends in England who have provided the means of endowing this newly-constituted See of Montreal, than by endeavouring that the seed thus sown may, by God's blessing, produce the proper fruit.

While, however, we are all bound to seek to provide for the wants of our own people, and I must ever remember my duty to the Church of which I have been appointed a chief pastor and overseer, yet still I hope always to be able to cultivate a spirit of charity toward all around me; and if there be any rivalry with any of those who are members of other communities, I trust it will be only such a rivalry as shall lead each of us to strive who can most humbly and faithfully devote himself to the work of his ministry, seeking to cherish in the hearts of all who are under our care the purest principles of truth and piety.

On the following Sunday, being the 15th of September, 1850, the ceremony of the Bishop's enthronement took place at Christ Church, which thenceforward became the Anglican Cathedral of the diocese. The ceremony was described at length in the journals of the day, and included a notice of the Bishop's sermon preached on the occasion, from the text: "Lord, I will follow thee, whithersoever thou goest." It was commended for felicity of language and reverence of style, but especially for the preacher's modest and clear appreciation of the difficult duties of his exalted office. Besides the Bishop, four clergymen were mentioned as having been present at the solemnities of that Sunday service. The names are familiar names:

The Rev. JOHN BETHUNE, D.D., the Rector.
The Rev. Joseph ABBOTT, A.M.
The Rev. W. AGAR ADAMSON, D.C.L.
The Rev. D. ROBERTSON, A.M.

Most Rev. Francis Fulford, D.D.

With the exception of the Rev. John Bethune, who in point of years was the senior clergyman then present, all have departed this life. We may further add that three, namely: the Bishop, the Rev. W. Agar Adamson, and the Rev. D. Robertson, died within a period of less than two months of one another.

The grouping of these names recalls a circumstance with respect to one which, if we recollect aright, took place in the presence of all. The Rev. D. Robertson was at that time the resident chaplain of the forces at Montreal. He is remembered affectionately by the few who enjoyed his friendship, and kindly by many who possessed his acquaintance only. Though learned and charitable, he neither attracted followers nor won friends, for his great simplicity of character was controlled by a shyness of manner which repelled approach and made intimacy difficult. But though he was personally known to few, his figure, his dress, his gait, and his scrupulous regularity, made him for about thirty-five years a noticeable man in Montreal and Quebec. Change and decay touched him, and at last mortally; but they did their work within, for they produced less alteration than might have been expected in his outward appearance. They neither bowed his back nor blended grey with his brown hair. The older he grew the more upright he seemed to grow, and the conjecture arose that from constantly mixing with soldiers he had caught their style, and had come at last to look like them. His clothes, too, which were of the regulation pattern, had what the tailors call "a garrison cut." His coat, for example, was a severely military one, and had the allowance of collar which is usually bestowed on the tunic of a sergeant.

It was always "close buttoned to the chin," and naturally, for it had a warm heart to take care of. His hair sympathized with his attitude, for it was rigidly erect and shot upwards with "Excelsior" like determination, seemingly intent on getting as high as it could in the world. This peculiarity gave his head a broom-like appearance, which was not only in keeping with his figure, but supplies the point to the anecdote we are about to relate. A course of lectures was delivered in the Cathedral of Montreal, by clergymen who were chosen indifferently from various parts of the Province. Of the lecturers, one or two were Irishmen who had but lately arrived from their native land. "Irish divinity," as it was somewhat flippantly termed, was the particular stripe of divinity which one of the freshmen affected, who preached on the occasion to which we are about to refer. His sermon was an earnest composition, perhaps more conspicuous for freedom of expression than for exactness of thought. It was more florid than terse, and though not the style we should choose, it was nevertheless appreciated by the large class of listeners who relish a racy denunciation of all who do not think as they think, and talk as they talk. Mr. Robertson was a Scotsman by birth, educated, as we believe, at a Scotch university, and brought up, as we have heard, as a member of the Scotch Church. He was a keen thinker of the north country type, who cared little for words but much for ideas, who respected rather than trusted enthusiasm, and who wished that his religious life should be hedged with reason, or made plain by revelation. Nevertheless, some of the special doctrines of the church he had left were exquisitely painful to him, for, to use his own words, "his mind and heart recoiled from them." Now the Irish clergyman to whom we are referring particularly affected the very doctrines which distressed the Scotsman, and he dwelt on them, in his sermon, with a rapture which was rather aggressive than convincing. Mr. Robertson listened with as much patience as he could command, and rebelled as soon as an opportunity for doing so presented itself. When the service was over, and he could enter the vestry, he raised his hands, and with a droll Scotch emphasis addressed the Bishop, exclaiming, rather than saying : " My lord! my lord! when I heard such doctrine in a Church of England pulpit my hair fairly stood on end." But the excitement of a clergyman in a vestry, any more than the curiosity of a clergyman at a meal, did not throw the Bishop off his guard, for, with inimitable gravity, his Lordship looked at the incensed speaker, and said : " And I don't think, Mr. Robertson, it has gone down since!" The effect was as peaceful as the pantomime was droll, for the spirit of controversy was laid amidst irrepressible laughter; and thus the passing pleasantry very probably fulfilled the exact purpose for which the Bishop had made use of it.

On the 11th of October, 1850, being less than a month after his arrival at Montreal, the Bishop began to take measures for the systematic promotion of church work, and for such purpose the Church Society of the Diocese of Montreal was organized. The act by which that society was incorporated, though passed in the following session, was reserved for the signification of the Royal assent, but from some informality, the proclamation which authorized it to go into force was not made until the ninth of June, 1852. Between the passing of the act incorporating the Church Society and the time for its going into force, a circumstance of a somewhat embarrassing kind occurred which calls for a passing notice. The question raised seems to have included a conflict of ecclesiastical jurisdiction, of which the Bishop had received no previous intimation, and for which he had scarcely had an opportunity of sufficiently preparing himself.

On the 10th of October, 1851, a public meeting was held in the school room of St. George's Church, Montreal, for the purpose of forming an auxiliary branch of the "Colonial Church and School Society" of London, for the District of Montreal. This meeting supplemented proceedings commenced elsewhere, and those proceedings, as well as the meeting, seem, and as we think for sufficient reasons, not to have been satisfactory to the Bishop. This dissatisfaction became public on the sixth of the following month, when the Bishop addressed a letter to the clergy of his Diocese, in which he forcibly reviewed the rules and proceedings of the last mentioned society, and made some remarks that are worthy of being recalled, irrespective of their connection with the subject that gave rise to them. After saying, what indeed should never be overlooked, that the character and opinions of a Christian Bishop are the property of his diocese, his lordship observed that, before he left England, he called on his Metropolitan, the Archbishop of Canterbury, who sent him forth with many words of kindness, of counsel, and of blessing, exhorting him in these times of division and controversy "to be temperate in all things;" to strive to gather together in one the members of Christ's flock placed under his care, and to lead them on in unity of spirit, in the bond of peace, and in righteousness of life. And by way of illustrating his desire to act as his Metropolitan had advised, his lordship very properly referred to the addresses of the clergy and laity which had been presented to him on his arrival in Canada, as well as to his answers to those addresses; and then with excusable warmth continued: "I commenced with good faith my labours amongst you. I determined to be no party Bishop, to discountenance in every way a partizan spirit. You can form some judgment whether I have acted up to that determination. I hoped that by moderation, and temperate administration, and the exercise of charity, that much misunderstanding of one another might be removed; that good and earnest hearts, though not always agreeing in all particulars, might yet work together for the welfare of our common mother, and the salvation of men. Wherever I saw devotedness and piety, I wished to acknowledge and foster it, and to live amongst my clergy (as I told them in my answer to their address) 'in the closest relations of confidential intercourse and mutual regard!'"

Having stated that the special duties of a Bishop are "superintendence" and "oversight," his lordship observed that he had been selected by her Majesty, in the words of the patent of appointment, especially to exercise "jurisdiction and oversight;" that he had been consecrated to that end, and that he had solemnly promised with God's help to further that end in all true and honest ways. He then pointed out with considerable force what his objections were to the rules and proceedings of the Colonial Church and School Society, and closed his remonstrance thus:—

I have felt obliged for your sakes to speak somewhat of myself, but you will bear with me. I can assure you that I have not been hasty in deciding to take my present course in opposition to this society. I know the evil of controversy and the difficulties of contending even for the truth without losing our charity. I have wished to look to principles, not persons, and hope still to have kindly intercourse with those from whom I differ on this subject. May God give us all grace to act as becomes the gospel of Christ. I may possibly subject myself to the chance of being designated either here or elsewhere by names intended popularly to affix on me the stigma of a party, or identify me with those who are accused of being innovators or disturbers of the Church. I trust if this should be so, that it will not trouble you more than it will me. I appeal to twenty-three years' labour in the ministry, to the manner in which the services of the Church were conducted by me, and to the character I left behind me where I was known. You are judges of my course of action since I came into this Diocese. I have always laboured to uphold the truth as contained in the word of God, and taught by the Church, and quietly and soberly to act on her principles. He who does less is not faithful to his trust.

You must be fully aware that there are two distinctive principles connected with our communion, the Episcopate and the Book of Common Prayer. And in the Episcopate there are two elements—" orders" and " jurisdiction and superintendence." I honour sincerity and consistency in those who, dissenting from our communion, are faithful to their own principles. But if we ourselves consider our " orders " of no importance, allow Episcopal " jurisdiction and superintendence" to be over-ruled, and the Prayer Book superseded as our Service Book and rule of faith, what grounds of consistency, what bond of union remains ?

Whatever, then, may be the consequence, we must maintain each of these principles amongst ourselves, and act upon them. And if, in doing so, it shall happen that our good be evil spoken of, I only lament the fact as an unhappy sign of the times, but shall not be surprised; you will also weigh such conduct in the balance and estimate it at its intrinsic value.

If I have at all understood the temper of the clergy and laity during that free intercourse which I have had with them, during my tour throughout the Diocese, I believe that there are many with honest and true hearts, who, when they know the state of the question, will stand by their Bishop in opposition to any external usurped authority, come from what source it may; and to God's blessing I commend you and them, and all the brethren, and I ask your prayers. Anxious, to the best of my ability, by God's grace assisting me, to discharge faithfully the arduous ministrations of my high and responsible office, I fling myself unreservedly, as I feel I am justified in doing, upon that duty and affection which, as a Bishop and Chief Pastor of the Church of this Diocese, I have a right to claim from all the clergy and laity of our communion.

The remonstrance was so clearly and fairly put, that none could justly find fault with it. Indeed, it is scarcely to be supposed that any bishop, irrespective of his theological opinions, would have suffered, without protest, an act of ecclesiastical intrusion which would have neutralized his authority in his own diocese, and would for all practical purposes, as his lordship remarked, have "put the Episcopate in commission." The letter in many respects is a very interesting one, for while it enunciates true and sound principles, those principles are explained in the gentle language of one who strove for peace as well as for victory. A vain man would have been tempted to write in a different manner, for the case presented several particularly weak points and was fairly open to objection. But the Bishop was not indifferent to the fact that the object of the society was to do good. The diocese required all the help it could procure, for it stood in great need of clergymen, of schoolmasters and of books, and he was not the man to place uncalled-for impediments in the way of such work. Of what actually took place, we are unacquainted, but it is fair to assume that the Bishop's reasonable complaints were satisfactorily met, as his Lordship soon afterwards became, and we believe continued to the end of his life to be, the local President of that influential and popular society.

On the 20th January, 1852, a little more than three months after the correspondence to which we refer had taken place, the Bishop held a primary visitation of his diocese and delivered his primary charge. As we have elsewhere said, the clergy and laity, and especially the former, were a good deal exercised with respect to passing events in the church in England, as well as to their probable influence on the church in Canada. This circumstance, added to their desire to pay proper respect to their new Diocesan, may account for the fact that out of fifty-one officiating clergymen in the diocese, fifty were in attendance at the visitation. The charge, to the disappointment of some, who, in the words of an Irish clergyman present, had expected "materials for a difference," did not include any reference to those subjects which had occasioned much local disquiet; for, as another clergyman said to the writer on the occasion, "I was troubled when I went to the Cathedral on the subject of the Gorham controversy and the Surplice question, but I was consoled as I came away that our new Bishop left the first difficulty to the Ecclesiastical Courts and that he evidently did not care a button about the second!"

But if the charge was conspicuous for the absence of all allusion to certain topics, it is very noteworthy in its general character. If it struck a chord which in many subjects, did not harmonize with several preconceived notions, it nevertheless expressed opinions which we think had the merit of being accurate, and it sketched a policy which has not been wanting in success. With respect to a question on which much difference of opinion had previously existed, viz: *status* of the Anglican Church in Canada, the Bishop said:

It is my wish, in the first place, to direct your attention to the real position which, as members of the United Church of England and Ireland, we occupy in this Diocese. While, spiritually, we are identified with the Church in the mother country—emanating from her, using the same liturgy, subscribing the same articles, blessed with the same apostolic ministry—visibly forming part of the same ecclesiastical body, and claiming as our own all her mighty champions, confessors, and martyrs; yet, in a political sense, and as regards temporalities, and everything that is understood by a legal establishment, or as conferring special privileges above other religious communities, we are in a totally dissimilar situation.

Whether it ever was contemplated, in these respects, to carry out the theory of the Church of England in Canada, certainly it has never been practically effected. Politically considered, we exist but as one of many religious bodies, consisting of such persons as may voluntarily declare themselves to be members of our Church, and who thus associate together because they are agreed upon certain principles and doctrines according to which they believe it to have been from the beginning the rule of the Church to serve and worship God. The abstract truth of any religious principles or doctrine in no way depends on the degree of countenance which they may receive from the authorities of the State, nor can there be the slightest advantage or wisdom, but quite the reverse, in putting forward claims of the nature above mentioned, which we cannot fully substantiate, and which, circumstanced as we are here, if they were to be granted to us to-day, it must be absolutely absurd for us to expect to maintain.

But while we have been held to be identical with the Church in England, this practical and essential difference in our political and legal position has never been provided for, and the consequence has been that we have lost the administrative power provided for the

Church by its legal establishment at home, and none has been supplied adapted to our condition here. We seem to have been deprived of the ecclesiastical law of England, and have not been provided with any recognized and effectual means of self-government for those who associate themselves together as members of our communion in Canada. The only alternative has been to seek a remedy in the discretionary exercise of Episcopal rule and superintendence: an alternative which is not always available in all cases, and which by casting too much weight and responsibility upon the individual judgment and decision of the Bishop, has a tendency to deprive his decisions of much of that influence and authority which ought to attach to all the acts of the ecclesiastical body.

It cannot be thought unreasonable that we should all anxiously seek a remedy for this evil. It was a full consciousness of our unsatisfactory state, in this respect, that influenced the Bishops assembled at Quebec at our recent Episcopal Conference, when we unanimously agreed, amongst others, to a resolution expressing opinions almost identical with those which we lately embodied in the proceedings of our "Church Society" at one of the meetings of the Central Board, namely, "That in consequence of the anomalous state of the Church of England in these Colonies, with reference to its general government, and the doubts entertained as to the validity of any code of ecclesiastical law, the Bishops of these Dioceses experience great difficulty in acting in accordance with their Episcopal commission and prerogatives, and their decisions are liable to misconstruction, as if emanating from their individual will and not from the general body of the Church, and that, therefore, it was considered desirable that the Bishops, clergy, and laity of the Church of England, in each diocese, should meet together in Synod at such times, and in such manner, as may be agreed; the laity meeting by representation, and that their representatives must be communicants." I most firmly believe that a provision, such as is thus recommended, for the purpose of supplying sufficient means of self-government for the Church, (having reference, of course, only to those who, by voluntarily joining our communion, must necessarily be subject to its rules), would not only have the happiest influence on the Church at large, but would also strengthen the true and legitimate influence of the Bishop, and cause increased reverence and respect for his office and authority.

In England the Bishop had been minister of a church which is said to be fettered with privileges, and "in bondage to the state." Like many others, he had probably been of opinion that such privileges had proved of little service, and such bondage a great hindrance to her usefulness. Hence the absence of all connection of the church with the state in Canada, was a condition he could look at bravely and without trepidation, so far as the church was concerned, for he was not required to give any opinion on the involved point whether the state and not the church would be likely to suffer most by a separation. Apart from these considerations, the Bishop of Montreal differed from his Episcopal brother at Toronto, in his constitutional aversion to claim a doubtful right, or to insist on a disputed privilege. He would not appropriate as law that which was not clearly expressed in the law; neither would he take advantage of analogy, or strain unduly the application of a custom. This policy, which is generally the wisest, as well as the best, was attended with the usual results. Indifference on his part was rewarded with consideration on the part of those who would have resisted any pretension to privilege, and hence he received as marks of conventional courtesy what would have been withheld had his claims been founded on questionable rights. Consequently the Bishop won respect from all—from Roman Catholics, as well as from Protestants—by his declaration that the Church of England in Canada, politically considered, " exists but as one of many religious bodies," and therefore it was that all denominations of Protestants, with a unanimity amounting almost to enthusiasm, accorded to him the chief place in the religious and social community of Montreal. They yielded to his office a degree of respect which it had never before received, and which was scarcely inferior in affection to that which they were accustomed to pay to their more immediate pastors.

Having laid down the principle that the Anglican Church in Canada would win, rather than lose consideration, by claiming no doubtful privileges, his Lordship referred to the differences between the various religious communities, in the following suggestive words :

But we must look at the duties of the clergy, not only towards those within our own communion, but also towards those who are without. The visible unity of the body of Christ is marred by the sins and weakness of man ; and the unbeliever and the ungodly draw from thence much encouragement to gainsay the truths of revelation and the plain requirements of the law of God. If, therefore, the differences that exist between various religious communities are not thought of material importance, they must surely appear to us to be unjustifiable and sinful. If, however, we think ourselves justified in maintaining them, we ought to be fully persuaded in our own minds of the grounds upon which they are founded. But in all such questions let it be our care still to maintain our Christian charity ; to contend for truth, not for victory ; to condemn not persons, but their errors, and to be far more diligent in declaring positive truths, than in denouncing the belief or practice of our neighbours. A little religion is very apt to engender a violent spirit of partizanship ; a larger measure of grace and knowledge, while it confirms us in our own position on better and clearer grounds, teaches us also more correctly in what way we act towards other. "We have just enough religion," says an excellent author "to make us hate, but not enough to make us love one another !" If we establish truth, error will fall of itself, not immediately perhaps, but gradually and finally. Belief cannot be forced. To attempt it will only generate hostility. But by the exercise of Christian virtues, by upholding the truth with meekness and gentleness, by putting the most candid construction upon the motives of them that be in error, by inducing them to view the truth from other points than those to which education or habit have accustomed them; by such methods will the Christian religion be most successfully propagated.

If you endeavour to cultivate such a spirit, no one who is worth listening to will ever think the worse of you for being faithful to the specific principles of the communion to which you belong, or for being anxious to act up to the tenor of your ordination vows. Far otherwise. Be assured that your truth and consistency will gain respect and confidence; your Christian moderation and charity will win love and souls.

With respect to the authority under which the Pope had recently made several high ecclesiastical appointments in England, the Bishop expressed some noteworthy sentiments, and especially on the unwarranted usurpation, which the act implied, over all other churches by the Bishop of Rome; for the protest against such usurped power, as his Lordship elsewhere observed, was the first actual step, and, practically, the most important one, in the reformation of the English Church. In connection with this subject, and by way of illustrating it, some striking extracts are made from the apostolical letter of Pope Pius the ninth, re-establishing the Roman Catholic hierarchy in England, which may be read with advantage, since they corroborate an important truth of ecclesiastical history, and show that the Churches of England and Rome are in accord with respect to the existence of a duly constituted Christian church in the British Islands before the arrival of Augustine. After alluding to "the power of governing the Universal Church entrusted by our Lord Jesus to the Roman Pontiff," the letter sets forth that "the records of England bear witness that from the first ages of the Church, the Christian religion was carried into Britain, and that it afterwards flourished there very greatly, but that towards the middle of the fifth century, after the Anglo-Saxons had been called into that Island, not only the commonwealth, but religion also, was seen to fall into the most deplorable condition. But it is recorded that our most holy predecessor, Gregory the Great, immediately sent thither the Monk Augustine."

After speaking at some length on the argument by which the supremacy of the Pope is sought to be maintained, the Bishop refers, with commendable warmth, and in no doubtful language, to the two especial blessings which the Reformation has secured to us. "It is," said the Bishop, " the first great excellence of the Church to which we belong, that in all her formularies and articles, she shrinks from no enquiry, and fears no comparison with the written word. She says to all, 'Search the Scriptures to see whether these things are so.' The second great excellence is the Book of Common Prayer, for that wonderful compendium of Christian duty not only leads us with one mind and one mouth to worship God, but it provides us with confessions of faith and standards of doctrine, so that any devout person may search with some assurance of success for a knowledge of the truths that are revealed in the word, and preserved by the Church of God." By way of corroborative proof, the Bishop adduces, as was his frequent custom, the testimony of devout non-conformists to the value of "creeds, catechisms and confessions of faith;" the testimony on the present occasion is supplied by an extract from Baxter's catechism

What need we catechisms while we have the Bible?

Because the Bible contains all the whole body of religious truth which the ripest Christian should know, but are not all of equal necessity to salvation with the greatest points; and it cannot be expected that ignorant persons can cull out these most necessary points from the rest without help. A man is not a man without a head and heart, but he may be a man if he lose a finger or a hand, but not an entire man, or a comely man without hair, nails, and nature's ornaments; so a man cannot be a Christian, or a good and happy man, without the great, most necessary points in the Bible, nor an entire Christian without the rest. Life and death lieth not on all points alike, and the skilful must gather the most necessary points for the ignorant, which is a catechism.

But are not the articles of our Church, and the confessions of Churches their religion?

Only God's word is our religion as the Divine rule; but our confessions, and books, and words, and lives, show how we understand it!

With respect to Common Schools, the Bishop differed from his western brother, the late Bishop of Toronto, on the duty to be observed by the clergy and laity with regard to such schools. He did not content himself with abstract propositions, which may be as really impracticable as they are apparently true. He did not discuss principles which may be said to be incontrovertible. On the contrary, he spoke appreciatively on a very difficult subject, for he thought as a statesman as well as a divine, and he did not deem it unbecoming the sacredness of his order to extend sympathy and assistance to rulers constitutionally chosen, who were probably as earnest as he was in their desire to promote the happiness and welfare of the country. The Bishop did not require to be informed that Canada, with its distinctive populations, and its manifold forms of religious belief, was exactly the country in which the question of Common

School education could only be settled if settled at all, with difficulty and by compromise. His Lordship was alive to the fact that he had to deal with things as they were, and not with things as he might wish them to have been. We may yearn for better food than the land affords, but we are obliged to put up with such as we are able to obtain; and it is our duty to make the best use we can of it. The Bishop had to consider what was available and not only what was preferable. He had to accept what was possible, and to pray for what was best. The difficulty of a statesman was the opportunity of a bishop, not only, or chiefly, to magnify his office, but to show the wisdom and generosity of his church. Let us, the Bishop in effect said, not embarrass, but rather, if we may, let us help the government; let us show our anxiety to assist in the great work of educating the people, and not unfairly raise difficulties or objections because we cannot have everything settled after our own plans. Let us, as churchmen, do all we can effectively to promote the necessary work with whatever machinery the means at our disposal may furnish us, and let us rejoice to see that done by others which we cannot do ourselves, if only it be done sufficiently. 'In passing it may be well to remember that as all education is only relatively perfect, an imperfect education is better than no education at all, because partial knowledge is preferable to total ignorance.

Sympathy and co-operation on the part of the clergy in the cause of secular education, not only adds a purifying salt to such education, but by increasing the intercourse between the clergy and the laity, extends the influence of the ministers of Christ, and, it may be, adds to the charm and attractiveness of the blessed truths they are commissioned to teach. The Bishop courted rather than shrank from the responsibility of placing the church and her ministers in direct contact with secular teaching, for he knew that the pure doctrine of the former and the gentle influence of the latter would suffer nothing from such contact. Unlike the rod of Aaron, which destroyed rivalry by consuming rivals, the Anglican Church in the Bishop's opinion should overcome evil with good, and by the heavenly grace of charity deprive sectarian enmity of its sting, and thus move those who are separated from her to respect her character, even though they should decline to assent to her creeds. Therefore he sought for no separation of the schools for Protestants; he desired no special privileges for churchmen; and thus he won the respect of all, no matter whether they belonged to, or differed from the body of which he was a chief ruler. He had faith in his office and ministry, and all things being equal, he believed in the superior attractiveness as well as the ultimate triumph of his principles; for as he eloquently added:

If the present be with us in many ways a day of small things, it is also, I feel sure, a day of hope; if we are conscious of our weakness, we must only be led by it more earnestly in dependence on God's blessing, to seek to "strengthen the things that remain." But although we be little among the mighty gatherings of the people around us, yet have we the fellowship with the countless hosts whose tents are spread throughout all the world, and whose voices are heard in one united strain of prayers and praises in the courts of the Lord's house. The world is everywhere full of excitement, eager after progress, and pleased with novelty.

"Human kind rejoices in the might
Of mutability—"

But the Church of Christ, like her great Head, is, in all her great principles of faith and doctrine, the "same yesterday, to-day, and for ever." She may be rich or poor, settled, or missionary, persecuted by a Dioclesian or served by a Theodosius; but still her identity as a spiritual body is maintained, her faith unchanged, built upon the foundation of the apostles and prophets, Jesus Christ himself being the chief corner stone.

Such sentiments conciliated the respect and secured the support of generous men, and at the time of their delivery were of especial advantage to the state as well as to the church. The irritating ecclesiastical questions that had vexed the country for years, clamoured for settlement; and the time had come when, in the interest of morals and of religion, the irritation should be set at rest. Much was gained by the friends of peace and concord when a bishop from his cathedral throne could say that the Anglican Church in Canada possesses no political advantages over any other denomination, but "that we exist but as one of many religious bodies." This official renunciation on the part of the Bishop of all claim to privilege, materially strengthened his claim to what was right. Such liberals as Sir Louis Lafontaine and the Hon. Robert Baldwin cordially recognized the validity of such claim while Sir Francis Hincks, who certainly owed no goodwill to the church party, said, with characteristic energy, in his place in parliament, that he was resolutely "determined to do justice to the Church of England."

Chapter Third.

All extremes are error. The reverse of error is not truth, but error still. Truth lies between these extremes.

CECIL.

Moderation is commonly firm, and firmness is commonly successful.

JOHNSTON.

BISHOP FULFORD had now been sixteen months in his Diocese. From his correspondence with the representatives of the Colonial Church and School Society, people generally were made acquainted with the kind of liberties he would not allow. From his primary charge they were able to infer that on matters of principle he would be firm, and that on matters unessential he would be conciliatory, if not accommodating. It was clear the Bishop was prepared to tolerate in his diocese a healthy diversity of opinion. He had been no inattentive student of the signs of the times, and the result of such study had probably taught him that the age was too practical to be ruled by tradition and too impatient to be governed by routine. It was therefore evident that his Lordship would not vex the Church on matters indifferent, or require his clergy to walk in contracted grooves, for he had no desire to invite frivolous disputes or to excite fretful prejudices. There was work to be done of such magnitude as would overshadow all littleness, and it was to be done by a diversity of minds for a diversity of minds. Old notions had indeed undergone a strange change when from his Cathedral throne a Bishop appointed by the Crown could without qualification or regret declare that the Anglican Church neither possessed nor claimed any political privileges in Canada. The announcement may have surprised some, but it produced a salutary effect on all. A new energy became suddenly apparent throughout the diocese. The clergy and the laity seemed to shed their lethargy, and to act as if they had been provoked to "love and to good works." "If it be true," we can imagine them to have said, "that the Anglican Church has no better legal status than any other religious body in Canada, it is our duty with God's help, to improve her moral status, and by every fair and just means to win back to her care those, who but for her coldness never would have been estranged from her fold." Neither will it be out of place to observe that the complete local organization of the church, attended as it always is with greater force and better means for work, was followed with marked results. By the Census Returns of 1851, the Church of England population of Montreal is given at 3,993 of a population of 57,715, while in 1861, the numbers returned were 9,739 of a population of 90,320; or, deducting the Roman Catholic population, the number represented by members of the Church of England, as against all other Protestant bodies, will be found to be 3,993 against 16,251 in 1851, and 9,734 against 24,427 in 1861, being at the first period less than a fourth, and at the second more than a third of the whole Protestant population.

Among the early plans of usefulness which the Bishop endeavoured to carry out was the establishment, at Montreal, of a church school for girls, where the higher branches of education would be taught, and where the moral influence of the Church of England would be inculcated and enforced. The first adventure was not encouraging and several unforeseen difficulties appeared to stand in the way of a second experiment. The project, however, was one to which the Bishop attached great value, and which he probably would have revived had his life been spared. In the meanwhile the question of parochial organization in Montreal required to be dealt with, as it was at that time in an unsettled, not to say disputed condition. The resignation, consequent on the removal of the seat of government, of the eloquent Assistant Minister of the Cathedral, enabled the Bishop, with the help and cordial concurrence of the Rector, to make such arrangements with respect to the Cathedral staff as might be expected, in part at least, to promote the object he had in view.

It has frequently been observed as a weak point in the administrative system of that section of the clergy whom for convenience only we shall call " Evangelicals," that they are not understood by the poor, nor are they apt at parish work. For reasons which we think are sufficiently obvious, the tendency of their opinions, as well as of their system, is to separate rather than to combine ; to divide rather than to fuse ; to become congregational rather than parochial ; independent rather than catholic. This inclination is commonly spoken of as a fault, and by most thoughtful persons is regarded with regret. Unquestionably there are in Canadian towns reasons of a local kind which aggravate this admitted evil; and perhaps there were at the period in question special circumstances at Montreal that might have excused a special caution. It is probable that the Bishop observed a disposition on the part of some to fall into the error of those early Christians who were censured for their desire to "sit under" one Apostle rather than under another—to prefer Cephas to Paul or Paul to Cephas.

To correct what seemed to be inexpedient if not irregular, an effort was made to approximate more closely to the parochial system of the mother country. The clergy apparently became more impressed with the duty of taking the spiritual care of a district rather than with the duty of only devoting themselves to the spiritual comfort of a congregation; and perhaps, also, the laity became more alive to the convenience if not to the obligation of worshipping within the parish limits in which they lived, rather than of following their own fancies to distant and out of the way churches. For these amongst other reasons, Montreal was mapped out into ecclesiastical boundaries, and each district, thus divided was set apart as the conventional parish of the neighbouring church. To fulfil the work of the Cathedral parish more clergymen were required than had theretofore been attached to the parish church. A meeting was consequently held of the Rector and congregation, when an agreement was arrived at to appropriate annually from the Cathedral rent fund, a certain fixed sum to enable the Bishop to pay the stipends of two clergymen to be engaged by him. Thus it was that two gentlemen then doing duty in England, of great experience and ripe scholarship, were found to accept the offices which had been thus created. Those gentlemen were previously unknown to the

Bishop. They were chosen for and not by him. This fact, apart from all other considerations, was attended with several important advantages, for it showed that the choice was made irrespective of any other consideration than the fitness of the persons chosen.

And here it may not be out of place to remark that Bishop Fulford regarded his patent of appointment as a holy trust held for the benefit of the church, and not as a secular instrument for the preferment of his friends. Happily for him, and some will add, happily for the church also, that gifted Prelate was not indebted to popular suffrage for the place he had been called upon to fill. He received his credentials as he received his authority—from the higher powers; and that authority was associated with no other condition than "to act well his part." He had not stooped that he might rise, nor had he ever been accused of doing discreditable things that he might dispense honourable ones. He had not met stratagem with craft, or checked an unworthy contrivance with a contrivance less creditable. None could say that he had soiled the purity of his lawn by dragging it through the mire of an indecent contest, or had been affronted with the imputation of mortgaging patronage to win a mitre. Malice could not charge him with degrading his order by manœuvring for votes or with gaining one step to his throne, as a huckster does a bargain, by haggling for conditions. He had not been required to discipline his mind to the composition of canvassing circulars, neither had he found occasion to use his hands in circulating addresses, calculated to depreciate the influence of any member of his cloth. He had not been reproached for making substantial equivalents for spiritual services, neither had he been blamed for entering into special covenants for the advancement of his friends. He had no indescribable kindnesses to recompense and no favoured party to reward; no supporters to smile upon and no opponents to slight. No intangible fetters chained him, neither was he straightened by imperceptible bonds. He was free from obligations to active committees; and though he could not expect to escape from importunity, he had not rendered himself liable to reward it. Being upright in conduct, pure in intention, and unfettered in judgment, he was in the condition to do as he thought best, and to render justice to all. If he erred in dispensing his patronage, his errors were those of one who had possibly exaggerated the meaning of the parting counsel of his Metropolitan, the Archbishop of Canterbury, who earnestly advised him to be neither the bishop of a party nor the patron of a sect. So thoroughly did he shrink from the humiliation of such reproaches, that, in his anxiety to avoid them, he ran some risk of falling into the opposite error; for, in the opinion of some, he pursued the common state policy of propitiating opponents at the expense of friends, and thus of inviting the imputation of acting weakly, if not partially; for it is alleged, that he bestowed the greater number of his favours upon those with whom he least sympathized, and whose views on many subjects were not in correspondence with his own. Thus, for example, clergymen in Canada whose theological notions are most in accord with the opinions of the particular party in the Church at home whose mission in Ireland has been stigmatized as a failure, found easy access to many of the best places, as well as to some of the highest honours of his diocese. Such a policy, view it as we may, is fairly open to criticism, while its probable consequences could not fail to occasion great anxiety to some of the most earnest members of the Church. Nevertheless a prelate who thus acts, wins a repute for fairness if not for wisdom; and at least, secures himself from the miserable imputation of making his opinions the law of the Church, and his prejudic the measure of that law. As a matter of principle and apart from all considerations of policy, even had his powers been absolute, the Bishop would probably have pursued a course on the subject of patronage different only in degree from the one he adopted. His large and philosophic mind found no pleasure in crippling Christian freedom or in narrowing Christian fellowship within limits less comprehensive than the Prayer Book allows. Hence he not only admitted the fact of a diversity of views, but, if we mistake not, he recognized an advantage in the existence of such a diversity. In the words of St. Paul, he might have said "though I be free from all men, yet have I made myself servant unto all, that I might gain the more."

While maintaining her principles in the broadest and most comprehensive sense, the Bishop was apparently of the opinion that a National Church should adapt her organization to the condition of the nation; and, subject to the divine law, be " all things to all men." He knew that the middle place in catholic christendom held by the Anglican Church was, so to speak, the place of charity as well as of truth. Removed from the Latin Church on one hand and from the non-conforming bodies of Christians on the other, she nevertheless holds a position relative to both.

Therefore it was matter of rejoicing and not of disquiet to him to observe one section of his clergy, in the language of Keble, "speaking gently of their sister's fall," and by tender love striving "to win the Romanist back again to the better part," and to see another section of his clergy stretching out a sympathetic hand towards their separated Protestant brethren, and by every tender endearment alluring them to the "rock whence they are hewn." There can be little doubt that the Bishop wisely recognised, in the action of both parties, the great scriptural duty of drawing all men "by the unity of the same spirit" towards the common "path of peace."

But to return to our narrative. The clergymen who had been invited to join the Cathedral staff of the diocese soon afterwards arrived at Montreal. They were the Reverend Henry Martyn Lower, M.A., and the Reverend Samuel Gilson, M.A. Both were at once appointed Canons of the Cathedral, while, by way of addition, the former was created Archdeacon of the diocese. They became as we have been informed fast friends of the Bishop, as well as fellow-workers with the clergy of the diocese. Subsequently the Rev. Mr. Lower was connected with his Diocesan by nearer ties, for he married Alice Fulford, the Bishop's only daughter. Those gifted clergymen need no praise of ours, indeed praise would be distasteful to them and out of place in this sketch, but they must forgive the writer for recording the deep regret which was, and is, felt by many that by reason of their return to England, their zeal, learning, and example are no longer the property of the Canadian Church.

Like the present Dean of Chichester, the Rev. W. F. Hook, and many besides, the Bishop had broken away, so to speak, from the traditional routine which had too commonly been observed by the English clergy, for he was keenly alive to the duty of doing and of aiding others to do all possible good. It is difficult for an earnest man to look abroad without observing that outside of the customary modes, and away from the beaten tracks of benevolence, there is much work to be done—much kindly, charitable, helping work that a Christian minister might and could do without rendering himself liable to the rebuke of being unfaithful to his calling or false to his vows. The Bishop knew what his church required of him, and he observed her requirements, but he also knew that beyond the strict limits of his profession he might accomplish much useful work —such work as a good subject and a charitable citizen, irrespective of his religion or calling, might successfully perform. Hence he cheerfully co-operated with all societies and associations that were established for benevolent, scientific, philanthropic or useful purposes. He wrote papers for and devliered lectures to, mechanics at their institutes, to library associations at their rooms, and to working men at their clubs. Several papers were printed and are very interesting. Thus we find that the mechanics of Montreal were favoured with some very thoughtful remarks on Colonial Institutions. The Natural History Society of Montreal had the advantage of a paper on the state and prospects of science and literature in that city. The Diocesan Library Association was counselled on the subjects of taste and style in literature, and the Church of England Association for Young Men, besides several other lectures, was edified with some recollections of a visit to Abbottsford and of Sir Walter Scott and his contemporaries, while the Churchman's Association of Montreal was instructed on some of the passing events and controversies of the day. These papers are mentioned for the convenience of illustration only, and by way of affording our readers some acquaintance with the subjects on which the Bishop chose to treat. But while they supply references to his Lordship's manner of thought, they give no idea of the number of papers, speeches and addresses which he was constantly called upon to deliver and which he did deliver with cheerfulness and good will.

Another illustration of what some considered the Bishop's policy, but what we prefer to call his wisdom, is associated with the history of the Montreal Cemetery for the interment of Protestants. In other places in Canada, different denominations of Protestants possess, as at Toronto, separate places of burial; or as at Quebec, one place of burial with border lines dividing those who sleep in consecrated from those who sleep in unconsecrated ground. Both arrangements present some sentimental, and many practical disadvantages, for they separate in death those who lived together, and were probably related to one another in life. The Bishop appears not to have recognised a necessity for such separations; and therefore, when the Montreal Cemetery was set apart for the burial of the dead, his Lordship won golden opinions for himself and for his church by suggesting, or by acting on the suggestion of others, that denominational distinctions should not be perpetuated in the grave, but that the whole enclosure should be peacefully dedicated to one common purpose, and solemnly consecrated in accordance with the form and ceremonial of the Anglican Church. Many, no doubt, have visited, and will visit, that place of beauty where their departed friends sleep. If, when doing so, they should stand beside the good Bishop's grave, they may observe, hard by, the monument of one, a member of the Church of Scotland, who loved the English Prelate in life as one friend loves another, and who was happy to know that in death he would rest beside him in kindred earth, for the adjacent column of Aberdeen granite preserves the familiar and unforgotten name of the Honourable Peter McGill. Not far removed the visitor will see other monuments whereon are chiselled other names; the names of men perhaps locally distinguished, whose "good deeds" are had in remembrance, and whose mortal remains— whether they be those of churchmen or nonconformists—rest side by side in adjoining graves, there to await their final summons to the great assize, when the issues of all controversy will be cleared up, and when wranglers and sophisters shall receive from the Great Teacher their befitting prizes.

Personal character must and does tell at all times and with all classes. It is especially valuable in a mixed community, whose interests and feelings, whose enmities and prejudices, seem always to be mapped in sharp and angular lines. Under such circumstances, it is something to be thankful for when the clergy are fair in repute, just, honest and of good report; when their characters are without warp and their transactions without stain, and when straightforwardness of conduct is written in every passage of their lives. Such an one was the late Metropolitan, and consequently he received the esteem and respect of all, from the working man, who revered him for his sympathy with working men, to the most vehement opponent of his Episcopal rule, or the most conscientious separatist from the Episcopal Church. For although a Bishop cannot and ought not, on subjects of religion and orders and worship, to discredit his vows, or to make light of his oaths; though he ought not to associate ecclesiastically with those who deny the doctrine and disown the fellowship of his church, and being sincere and intelligent persons, acquainted with the subscriptions he has made and the obligations he has assumed, they would but lightly esteem him if he were to do so; still, on matters of a secular kind, on matters of benevolence, philanthropy, and science; in fact on all common ground, on all neutral ground, on all public ground, a Bishop may, and we venture to think should, co-operate cordially with those among whom his lot in life has been cast. There can be very little doubt that before Bishop Fulford landed in Canada he had thoughtfully considered the moral chart of his diocese, and the result very probably found expression in his answer to one of the congratulatory addresses which were presented to him on his arrival at Montreal, where he stated: "That while we are bound to seek to provide for the wants of our own people, and I must ever remember my duty to the Church of which I have been appointed a chief pastor and overseer, yet still I hope to cultivate a spirit of charity to all around me." In this spirit of charity he diligently sought

> To lead the ages' great expansions,
> Progressive circles towards thought's Sabbath rest;
> And point beyond them to the many mansions
> Where Christ is with the blest.

And such was his aim to the last. Animated by the sense of duty rather than by the spirit of enthusiasm, he steadily pursued his course of wisdom and moderation with firmness and success. To those who seemed to be chiefly anxious to convert the French Canadian population, from the grave errors of the Church of Rome, he had some cautions to utter. The words of advice are repeated from memory: "Be careful how you destroy the hereditary religion of a people, and before you do so, be well assured that such people are in a condition to receive something better than that which you take away!" The Bishop especially inculcated the duty of performing every religious work in a religious manner; for religious and not for political ends. Therefore it was matter of small comfort to him that an individual forsook the religion of his fathers, if at the same time he did not become more humble, more charitable and more Christ-like. The conviction that only reaches to the head did not satisfy the Bishop who taught that religion was intended to cleanse and purify the heart. For knowledge without practice, like faith without works, is calculated rather to provoke satire than to produce thankfulness. Such intellectual properties, an old writer observes, "may do good to others, as the knowledge of Noah's carpenters was useful to him, while they perished in the flood!" But while the Bishop cautioned those whose missionary zeal was directed chiefly towards the conversion of Roman Catholics, he had some sound words of advice for those who were chiefly bent on exposing the errors of non-conformists. "In all such questions let it be our care still to maintain our Christian charity, to contend for truth, not for victory, to condemn, not persons but their errors, and to be far more diligent in declaring positive truths than in denouncing the belief or practice of our neighbours. A little religion is very apt to engender a violent spirit of partizanship; a larger measure of grace and knowledge, while it confirms us in our position on better and clearer grounds, teaches us also more correctly in what way we ought to act towards others."

The Bishop's writings should be in the hands of all—his sermons, lectures, and addresses, abound with fresh thoughts, while their style and tone are vigorous and manly, as if they had been beaten on the anvil of experience with the hammer of observation. He had the statesman's gift of being able to adapt his words to every kind of audience. He seemed to be equally at home when speaking to learned and scientific societies, to merchants or working men, to mechanics or soldiers, to youth at their colleges, or to the young of both sexes at the holy rite of confirmation. On such an occasion, after explaining the nature of the rite and what was expected of those on whose heads his hands were about to be laid, the Bishop thus concluded his address to the candidates in Christ Church Cathedral, on Sunday, the 7th February, 1864:

And who, and what are you that are thus about to draw so nigh to God, in the way which He has appointed? Born into a world of sin, with a fallen nature and a perishable body, you are nevertheless created for eternity. But an eternity of what kind; and where to be passed? It was to redeem you when in bondage, and save you when lost, that Christ took on himself our nature and sanctified it; and by His death for sin, who knew no sin, purchased the gift of eternal life for us. To Christ you were all dedicated at your baptism; and by His spirit a seed of this better life and sanctified nature was implanted within you. Shall that seed be nurtured, that it may grow and bear its proper fruit unto God? Or shall it be stolen away by the devil, or trodden under foot, or choked amidst the thorns and briers of this naughty world? Christ invites you to come to Him for safety and for succour, as He is set forth the one Mediator between your God and you. And it is in and by this ordinance of Confirmation, that you are to hope and believe, that, having been already enrolled amongst the soldiers of the Cross, you will receive strength to war a good warfare, and gain still closer union with Christ, with a confirmation of the Divine promises to you, even as you are now to confirm and renew your vows and promises to God. So also in prayer at all times, private or family prayer, public worship, in secret searchings of heart, patient submission to the will of God, and the earnest endeavour to obey him,—these are ways in which we shall all continually find our union with Christ—our inner life, which must all depend on Him,—strengthened and matured. But as the chiefest of all, in the holy Communion of His Body and Blood,—which blessed Sacrament was ordained, as you have been taught in your Catechism, "for the continual remembrance of the sacrifice of the death of Christ, and of the benefits which we receive thereby." And on Sunday next there will be a special early celebration of that holy Sacrament in this Cathedral, at nine o'clock, in order that any of those this day confirmed may so draw nigh to God, in that ordinance, for "the strengthening and refreshing of their souls by the Body and Blood of Christ," as our bodies receive strength from bread and wine. There will also, no doubt, in all the Churches, be early opportunities for all of you thus to draw nigh to Christ,—doing, what He has invited us all to do, in remembrance of Him. You will all, from this day, have the privilege of joining with the faithful wherever you may be, in this commemoration of Christ's precious death, and partaking of those good things thereby provided for them that love Him.

And oh! my young friends, just entering, as so many of you are, upon the serious trials of the battle of life, think what a privilege, what a comfort it must be to be allowed to fight that battle in the name and the strength of the Lord Jesus Christ, who says of Himself,—" Fear not; I am the First and the Last; I am He that liveth, and was dead; and behold I am alive for evermore, Amen; and I have the keys of hell and of death."

May you all steadfastly fight under His banner against sin, the world, and the devil; and, as was prayed for you at your baptism, " may you continue His faithful soldiers and servants unto your live's end." And as looking upon each one of you, now presented to me for my prayers and my blessing, as mine own child, as being your spiritual father in God, and your Bishop, I would say to each individual amongst you:

> " O my lov'd child, thou object of my care,
> How shall I hide thee from the unpitying winds
> Of this rude world; and thy cheek so fair
> In the sweet innocence of unsoil'd minds,
> From that which, ah! too soon the spirit finds?
> If I do love thee with a spirit's love,
> In this bad earth, where sin our vision blinds,
> How should I pray some Angel from above
> May guide thee from this world, and thy sure guardian prove."*

We have said elsewhere that the Bishop was no slave to routine, that he appeared indifferent on matters to which some persons attach importance. He was singularly apt in adapting himself to circumstances, and of being "all things to all men," if by any means he " might save some." Anecdotes illustrative of this peculiarity of his character are occasionally told, and especially with respect to incidents that took place in the more remote parts of his diocese. We cannot undertake to repeat what occurred in the words of our informants, and hence what we are about to narrate, must be received with a certain amount of qualification, as we

---

* " The Baptistery." Image VI. Childhood at Self-Examination.

give our impression of the story and not the words of the story. As an Englishman fresh from the metropolis, some of the clergy at first thought the Bishop would be a strict disciplinarian in the matter of ritual, and that lawn sleeves and lavender gloves would, in his person, make themselves conspicuous on all possible occasions. A very earnest, humble-minded and hard-working missionary was thus impressed when, for the first time, the Bishop was his guest:

"I like your Sunday service, it is simple and hearty," observed the Bishop to the Missionary.

"Ah, my lord," was something like the answer, "here, where I live, I am Mr. Rubric, but at my outlying stations I am Mr. Latitude, perhaps your Lordship would call me Mr. License. This is my model Church and my model service, and I am working in the hope of bringing the others up to it." Now Mr. Rubric, as we shall for convenience call him, had four or five stations. Where he lived, the Church was finished, and the services were, as we have reason to think, quite worthy of the commendation they received. Parenthetically we may mention that the surplice was worn throughout the service. But the outlying parts of his mission were new and wild, and the people for the most part were little acquainted with any special form of religion, and generally called themselves Protestants. Unquestionably they knew less of the worship of the Anglican Church than of the worship of any other Christian body. Mr. Rubric, out of respect to the prejudice of some who had never seen a surplice used in public worship, as well as from regard to the wish of others that the parson "should not be dressed like other folk," performed the whole of the service at one of his stations in a black gown. At a third, he neither wore gown or surplice; while, at a fourth, he shut his eyes like a puritan and prayed the Church prayers, which he had committed to memory, with his prayer book closed. "These people," he observed to the Bishop, "know nothing of the Prayer Book, and have only heard extempore prayer. Moreover, they are prejudiced on the subject of forms and are wholly ignorant of liturgies. They will not respond in the Litany or repeat alternately the verses in the Psalms, therefore I omit the former and read the latter throughout. In the meanwhile I am trying to teach them, for they are not worse than were the people at my other stations when I began, and I think I am making progress." "And I shall not interrupt your work, Mr. Rubric," said the Bishop, "but don't you ask me to approve of it officially, and I hope no one else will ask me to condemn it officially."

The Bishop's policy, if we may so term it, was preserved; but his plans were seriously interrupted. While he was quietly but systematically making arrangements and bending influences for more effectually carrying forward church work in his diocese, one of those unlooked-for events took place which go far towards destroying the best laid plans, for Christ Church, the Cathedral Church of his diocese, was wholly consumed by fire. The work of destruction was so complete that it became necessary to build afresh. For several reasons it was deemed expedient not only to select a new site, but to determine that the new structure " should be beautiful exceedingly," a visible commentary on the words of Solomon, when he said, " the house which I build is great, for great is our God above all gods." On the 21st of May, 1857, it was the Bishop's privilege to lay the foundation stone of the new building—a work which, in days future, will probably be regarded as a monument to the memory of the first Bishop of the diocese and of the first Dean of the Cathedral of Montreal. On Advent Sunday, 1859, he had the happiness to preach the opening sermon. It is not necessary to make any lengthened reference to the impediments, including the death of the architect, which, in several forms hindered the progress and increased the cost of the building. It is enough to observe that, between the estimates and expenditure, an unusual difference was found to exist, which necessarily weighted the new work with an oppressive debt, and, as a matter of course, damped the ardour, while it occasioned a ceaseless drain on the resources, of those who worshipped within its walls. This debt pressed heavily on the mind of the Bishop, and on many besides, who, with him, were more immediately responsible for its contraction. Like most English clergymen, the Bishop was not practically conversant with the popular modes of collecting money, and he was, on that account, the more discomforted when brought face to face with the kind of responsibility which the deficiency represented. The debt, it is true, was unavoidably incurred, but how to pay it was a question, the solution of which gave him serious anxiety. Apparently, his experience taught him but one way, and he determined, so far as he was concerned, to adopt that way. It was the old way of saving and of sacrifice, of contracted expenditure, and of household retrenchment, of patient thrift and practical economy. Such a way, though but slightly lightened by sentiment, was made attractive by duty. Wherefore he moved to a small dwelling, and laid aside not only every indulgence, but almost every convenience. His new mansion was modest enough, for it was built for the official residence of the parish schoolmaster. To be sure it adjoined the school-house, and consequently when in fulfilment of the duties of his office, the Bishop thought fit to show hospitality, the schoolrooms became his salons for the reception of his guests. And they suited the purpose very well, for they were airy and spacious apartments, whose whitewashed walls were pleasantly relieved with scrolls and maps, that served for ornament, instead of pictures and statuary, and though less beautiful were probably much more instructive. The illuminated texts and mottoes that adorned the cornices or festooned the windows, and were designed to furnish moral and religious axioms for the guidance of children, fulfilled the duty of reminding children of larger growth of what they were once taught and what they still might remember with advantage. Those days and months and years of sacrifice, we cannot doubt, were lightened with the holy exercise of faith and hope and prayer, for, like most honest exertion, they were followed by reward at last. One of the great purposes of the Bishop's life was fulfilled ere that life was closed; for if we are rightly informed, the Cathedral debt was paid before he died.

Churchmen of the present and of future times, as they look at or worship within that grand Anglican freehold, will gratefully remember the patient labours of Bishop Fulford, the cheerful energy of Dean Bethune, and the crowning exertions of Canon Balch. And it may be that some, at least, among those worshippers, on the Sundays and Holy-days to come, as they offer up the prayer for the "whole state of Christ's Chuch militant here on earth," will pause for a moment to point their thoughts as they recall the piety of the worthies of other times, and then, with a deeper reverence, ask for grace so to follow their good example "that, with them, they may be partakers of the heavenly kingdom."

In the last book which the Bishop published, a lithograph of CHRIST CHURCH CATHEDRAL, Montreal, is introduced by way of frontispiece. The fact is suggestive as well as appropriate, for such an illustration of one of the great purposes of his life is fittingly placed at the front page of his latest work. Though the site of the Cathedral is ill adapted to display the fine proportions of the building, yet the building itself is beautiful for elevation, while its contrasted masonry of gray and white sandstone, rich with corbels, and carvings, and fretwork, bear fitting testimony to the unity of the artist's plan as well as to the completeness of the builder's work. The exquisite spire rising skywards, like the monument of a saint, is well adapted to excite serious and awaken slumbering thoughts. The delicacy of its design, the harmony of its proportions, and the Mosaic brilliancy of its contrasts, captivate the imagination and exact tribute from the mind. It is beautiful to behold when bathed with "the gay beams of lightsome day," but it is glorious to gaze upon when the city sleeps, in the hush of night, when the stars are brightest or when the moon is abroad. At such a time, when all is still, the whole building seems to be spiritualized, and capable of stirring the deepest feeling. It suggests holy musings, recalls saintly memories and creates heavenly hopes. Thus may this mute minister prompt successive generations to consider the "living stones" of which that Temple is built that is "not made with hands." Thus may this monument of the just, point its "silent finger to the sky," and with even more than a preacher's power, direct wayward youth, ambitious manhood, and enfeebled age, to the life beyond life, the source of virtue, and the end of toil.

Chapter Fourth.

> Even so, the course of prayer who knows?
>   It springs in silence where it will,
>   Springs out of sight, and flows
>   At first a lonely rill:
>
> But streams shall meet it by and by
>   From thousand sympathetic hearts,
>   Together swelling high
>   Their chant of many parts.
>
> <div align="right">KEBLE's <i>Christian Year</i>.</div>

PEOPLE of a speculative turn of mind will have arrived at certain conclusions on the tendency of the age to accomplish purposes, small and great, by union and co-operation. Illustrations might be supplied in the history of commerce; in the manner in which profitable undertakings are carried out by limited partnerships or by joint stock companies, as well as by the more recent policy of amalgamating such companies. Or again such illustrations might be supplied in the history of nations, as in Europe, where the larger absorb the smaller states because such acts gratify a personal ambition or promote a traditional policy; or as in America, where the people are accustomed to think it is their destiny to acquire and possess a continent. Thus, to unite the States of Northern Germany under the Prussian rule, a frightful conflict was carried to a successful issue. In like manner, to preserve the unity of the States that control one half of the North American continent, a civil war, the like of which history furnishes no example, was waged with relentless violence to a victorious close. So also, in the other half of the same continent, negotiation was sagaciously employed to prevent provinces that were independent from continuing so any longer. War on one side, and legislation on the other, served the like purpose, for either they preserved or they promoted union.

In like manner, the moral and religious world appear to teach similar lessons. Christian denominations, for example, whose system, as their names import, is based on independence and isolation, have found solace, if not advantage, in forming themselves into "Congregational Unions." So also two or three branches of the Methodist body, and, if we are not misinformed, of the Baptist body also, which had separated from their respective roots and threatened to grow apart, have gently been entwined afresh within the branches of the parent tree. Neither may the rupture of the Scotch Church be regarded as a reason for setting aside the lesson of the age, for, in Canada at least, one effect of the Edinburgh schism has been to draw together, in one body, Presbyterian denominations which, but for that schism, would in all probability have continued in a state of obstinate separation. The newly constituted Presbyterian Church of Canada already includes the Free Church as well as the Relief and Secession Churches of Scotland. These represent fragments of such magnitude as almost to outweigh the Established Church of Scotland, from which they fell away; while, in the opinion of some persons, they constitute the numerical influence, if not the controlling power, of what once was an undivided Church. Neither is the prospect wholly chimerical that Canada may give lessons to the Church of Scotland in the matter of union as well as to the Church of England in the matter of discipline, for the desire exists, and is daily gaining strength in the minds of many of the members of the former establishment in Canada, that the breach of the eighteenth of May, 1843, should and may be repaired by extending the union which has already taken place, in such a way as to include, as the phrase is, "every orthodox type of the Presbyterian family."

With respect to the subject more immediately under our notice, it is probable that no collect, in these later days, has more frequently been used by devout members of the Anglican Church than THE PRAYER FOR UNITY with which we have prefaced this memoir. Nor by them only, for the spirit of that prayer has pervaded the devotions of multitudes who are neither members of the church, nor natives of the country, where the language is spoken in which that collect is written. In the Eastern Church and in the Western Church, amidst the fastnesses of Russia and within the shores of Sweden, over the plains of Germany and on the seven hills of Rome, by the Sleave and the Scandinavian, by the Teuton and the Frank, similar yearnings have been felt, and similar supplications have been expressed. The subjugating Anglo-Saxon family, in like manner, has very earnestly been moved towards the same object. In the United States as well as in the British Islands, in Canada and in the West Indies, in India and Australia, along the shores of the Pacific and amidst the islands of Oceanica the prayer for peace and concord has arisen to Him who is not only the "Author of Peace but the Lover of Concord." Under various names, but with one object persons have formed themselves into societies for the devout purpose of uniting their earnest prayers, with their earnest efforts, to bring about that day when men shall be of one mind, and when "the vexation of Judah" and "the envy of Ephraim" shall trouble the earth no more.

Nor are such hopes chimerical, for, whether whispered in the closet or uttered in the church, whether spoken in the broken accents of village worship or chanted with the harmonious accessories of a grand ceremonial, those prayers seem not to have been offered in vain. "The great searchings of the heart," that are everywhere apparent, have not been without their influence in British North America, where the growth and expansion of the Anglican Church have become studies elsewhere than in those Provinces; for men of earnest thought are endeavouring to apply in the Old World the instructive lessons that are being taught in the New.

Until a comparatively recent period, the Episcopal Church in America was really "without form or comeliness," a mere shrivelled offshoot of the Mother Church of England. Her despairing members and her scattered ministers must have been bowed down with discouragement or overtaken with despair, as they contemplated the imperfect nature of her organization. Then, as now, there were people who earnestly believed the early Christian adage of "No Church without a Bishop," and being consistent they must have been beset with doubts as to the existence of the former in a land where the latter was never seen. The members of the

Church must have felt the irony as well as the contradiction of the injunction which the minister was required to give when he baptized a child. How idle his exhortation to parents and sponsors to bring the newly "made heir of everlasting life" to the Bishop to be confirmed by him when no record existed that a Bishop of the Church of England had ever trod the shores of America, and moreover, when little hope was felt at that day that a Bishop ever would do so. For what do we see? While the Church of England requires in England three times the number of Bishops that she now has, and can neither get one from the state nor obtain leave to elect one for herself; neither could the Province of Canada for the period of eighty-five years after the conquest, obtain the assent of the Government to the appointment of more than one Bishop, or for the creation of more than one Diocese, in a territory whose limits extended from the Gulf of St. Lawrence to the Great Lakes, and from the Great Lakes to the Pacific Ocean. But as we have had occasion to observe elsewhere, the "day star" at length appeared, for in the second quarter of the present century a miraculous revival of church thought took place in England, and one of the earliest forms of its development was seen in the united efforts of all parties to increase the Colonial Episcopate, and thus add strength and stability to the Colonial Church.

When the first meeting for this purpose was held at Willis' Rooms, in 1841, there were but ten Bishoprics, throughout the Colonial Empire of England. At the close of 1867, or in twenty-five years, the number of Bishops, including five who were superannuated, had increased to fifty-six. But the movement contained a further principle of life. It not only increased the Episcopate, but it included results which few at that time had the penetration to foresee, and perhaps still fewer had the sagacity to carry out.

To gather parishes into dioceses with Bishops resident in each, was an inexpressible blessing to the church, for it provided for the distinct unity of the independent parts which compose a Christian Province: nevertheless, the organization continued imperfect, inasmuch as there were no means by which those parts, through their ecclesiastical representatives, might be brought together as one whole. Hence, as parishes had been gathered into dioceses, so, also, was it necessary to gather dioceses into Provinces, for in the absence of such a provision, the Colonial Bishops could only be regarded as Suffragans of the Archbishop of Canterbury, with the drawback of being practically beyond his observation and control. Thus, while the authority of the Colonial Bishops in their respective Sees was really absolute, it was virtually irresponsible, with the danger of becoming contradictory or opperssive. Appeals to a Moderator so distant as the Primate of England were scarcely to be looked for, and wrongs which might have been redressed on the spot, had a proper tribunal existed, were not redressed at all, because the court of ultimate jurisdiction was considered to be almost beyond reach. But, besides these practical objections, there were reasons in principle of a very grave character, that could not be overlooked. A condition of vassalage on the part of the Bishops of a separate Province to the Primate of England in some sort resembled the fealty which was exacted of their predecessors, in less happy days, by the Bishops of Rome; and, consequently the condition of dependence differed only in kind from the dependence which the Anglican Church disavows, and against which she has recorded her emphatic protest.

At the period we refer to, the Bishop of Toronto having proved himself to have been one of the most conscientious and law-abiding subjects in the Queen's dominions, suddenly arrived at the conclusion that there was little virtue in the law, at least in so far as it related to matters ecclesiastical in Canada, and therefore, as we assume, he seemed inclined to favor an experiment of virtue without law. Had the Bishop been a politician, the assembly which, in obedience to his summons, was convened at Toronto in 1851, would have been regarded as one of those unconstitutional provisional Parliaments which go by the name of General Conventions. But although the Bishop of Toronto had long ceased to be a politician, the assembly which he called together was nothing else than an ecclesiastical convention of the like irregular character with the political conventions to which exception has been taken, a convention that fulfilled the duties, though it did not assume the name, of a Diocesan Parliament. The plan which the Bishop of Toronto adopted was a very simple one. The clergy were summoned to a visitation, and each Clergyman, having a cure, was invited to request two or three of his parishioners, being communicants, to accompany him. A little later in the same year, the Bishop of Quebec held a visitation of his Diocese, when a course similar to that which had been pursued in the Western Diocese, was adopted by him. The experiments were deemed sufficiently encouraging to become the basis of proceedings of a more definite kind. Accordingly on the 23rd of September of the same year, five of the seven Bishops of British North America assembled at Quebec, where they remained for a week closely engaged in conference on the affairs of the Anglican Church in British North America. The minutes of that conference, which were unanimously concurred in by the Bishops who were present, and were generally agreed to by those who were absent, contained the following Canon on

CONVOCATION.

In consequence of the anomalous state of the Church of England in these Colonies, with regard to its general government and the doubts entertained as to the validity of any general code of ecclesiastical law the Bishops of these Dioceses experience great difficulty in acting in accordance with their episcopal commission and prerogatives, and their decisions are liable to misconstruction as if emanating from their individual will and not from the general body of the Church. We, therefore, consider it desirable, in the first place, that the Bishops, Clergy and Laity of the Church of England in each diocese should meet together in Synod, at such times and in such a manner as may be agreed on. Secondly, that the Laity in such Synod should meet by representation, and that their representatives should be communicants. Thirdly, it is our opinion that as questions will arise from time to time, which will affect the welfare of the Church in these Colonies, it is desirable that the Bishops, Clergy and Laity, should meet in Council under a Provincial Metropolitan, with power to frame such rules and regulations for the better conduct of our ecclesiastical affairs as by the said Council may be deemed expedient. Fourthly, that the said Council should be divided into two houses, the one consisting of the Bishops of these several Dioceses, under their Metropolitan, and the other, of the Presbyters and Lay members of the Church assembled as before mentioned, by representation.

Upon these grounds it appears to us necessary that a Metropolitan should be appointed for the North American Dioceses.

Petitions were thereupon presented by the clergy and laity of Canada to the Imperial Parliament, praying for leave on behalf of the Anglican Church in Canada, to hold deliberative conventions for the management of her affairs. As usual, in matters affecting the interests of the Church, the House of Commons was unable to agree on any measure of relief, and although the effort was ably made for three successive sessions, it always resulted in failure. Such defeats did not discourage the Canadians, who, like their American neighbours, generally show great aptitude for overleaping technical difficulties, and for obtaining in substance what eludes them in form. As the Imperial Parliament would not pass a measure of relief, it was suggested by some persons that redress might be obtained from the Provincial Legislature, without reference to the Imperial Parliament. Other persons, who were accounted legal whips, succeeded in satisfying the Bishop of Toronto that the difficulties which stood in the way of holding "national and provincial Convocations of the Clergy did not extend to Diocesan Synods." These comfortable counsels strengthened the resolves of that indomitable prelate, for, in 1853, he summoned his Clergy to a visitation, charging them, as he had done in 1851, to bring representatives from their respective congregations with them. The summons was obeyed, and no time was lost by the delegates, who had possibly been made aggressive by resistance, in shewing their determination to back up their Bishop and, if possible, perfect what he had left incomplete. A resolution was thereupon introduced and passed, which declared the irregular gathering to be a regular Synod. The proceeding displayed adroitness, but it did not remove doubts, and hence the less adventurous advisers, who had questioned the necessity of an Imperial Act, but had counselled the procurement of a Provincial one, received marked consideration for their opinions, and in due time the "Act to enable members of the United Church of England and Ireland in Canada to meet in Synod," introduced by the Honourable Mr. De Blaquière and passed by the Provincial Legislature in 1856, was assented to by Royal Proclamation in 1857. That measure not only authorised the Bishops, Clergy and Laity to meet in their several Dioceses in Synods, but it gave them permission to meet in "General Assembly within this Province." The powers thus conferred included the right to appoint a Provincial Metropolitan in accordance with the recommendation of the Bishops at their Conference in Quebec in 1851.

In 1859 the Diocesan Synods of Quebec, Toronto and Montreal, being three out of four of the Canadian Dioceses, petitioned Her Majesty to appoint one of the Canadian Bishops to "preside over the General Assemblies of the Church in the Province." These petitions were received very graciously, and in 1860 letters patent were issued promoting the Right Reverend Francis Fulford, D.D., Bishop of Montreal, to the office of Metropolitan of Canada, and elevating the See of Montreal to the dignity of a Metropolitical See with the city of Montreal as the seat of that See.

On the 10th of September, 1861, "The first Provincial Synod of the United Church of England and Ireland, in Canada, was begun and holden at the city of Montreal." To those whose hearts and minds had been earnestly bent on a closer union of all the dioceses of British North America, the occasion was one of personal as well as of historical importance. Assurances were furnished of the unity of the Canadian Church, while at the same time, no tie of affection was loosened which bound the daughter to the mother Church of England. But in setting up for herself, the Canadian Church very naturally looked about her for fellowship as well as for sympathy, and therefore, she made overtures of kindness, and sent messages of good will to her elder sister, the Episcopal Church of the United States. Thus Christian people who recognized the fact, as well as the necessity, of distinctions in the forms of civil government, nevertheless felt that there was a holier bond than that which civil government affords.

A more intimate fellowship with the Episcopal Church in America was a prospect full of actual and poetic interest. From their present elevation it was assuring to behold their future greatness. Christian philosophers of either country could, with equal satisfaction, trace the map from the sterile shores and frozen seas of the North, to the verdant landscapes and tepid waters of the Gulf of Mexico, and mark where it is dotted with the spiritual abodes of those who in doctrine, in orders, and in discipline are one with one another; who cherish the same pure Bible, the same reformed faith, the same ritual, the same creeds, the same sacraments, the same blessings in this life, and the same promises of reward in the life to come. No doubt it was a high honour which befell the Right Reverend Francis Fulford, when he was appointed Primate of the new ecclesiastical Province. It was moreover a congenial duty he performed when as President of the House of Bishops, he affixed his signature to the fraternal address which was adopted by the Provincial Synod, to the "Bishops, Clergy and Laity of the Protestant Episcopal Church of the United States of America assembled in General Convocation." The wish lay near his heart, for that heart was full of charity, and the prayer, there is reason to believe, was often on his lips, for those lips were much used to pray, that by the visible union of Christ's body upon earth the world may see and know "how good and pleasant a thing it is for brethren to dwell together in unity."

On the fourth of October, 1865, the Metropolitan of Canada had the privilege of preaching the sermon before the Protestant Episcopal Convocation which assembled at Philadelphia. From that sermon we extract the following words as illustrating the Bishop's sentiments on the point we have just noted:

A stranger as I must be to those intenser emotions with which you have all been affected, I yet claim to have the deepest interest in all that concerns your branch of the Church of Christ. And I claim this not merely as administering a diocese immediately bordering on your own, not merely as enjoying with all my brethren a communion with you in one common faith and ministry, but on grounds special to myself, and which I think over and above every other reason, and as it were actually identifying me with yourselves justify my being permitted the unusual privilege of occupying my present place a this most important occasion. And it is this, that nearly three quarters of a century after you had originally received your episcopate from our mother Church of England, I was the first Bishop of the Anglican Church that ever joined with your own Bishops in laying hands on any Presbyters about to be raised to the episcopate office among you, which I did in the case of the late lamented Bishop Wainwright, on which occasion I received a letter from one of your Bishops, present here this day, saying: "I esteem it no ordinary privilege to have been a participator in the first action by which the daughter and mother Church have reinosculated their succession. So that our Episcopacy receives a fresh communication of the Apostolic grace from the purest channel."

At the consecration of the Right Reverend Horatio Potter as Provisional Bishop of New York, in succession to Bishop Wainwright, on the 22nd November, 1854, the Bishop of Montreal preached the sermon from the text: "Holy Father keep through thine own name those whom thou hast given me, that they may be one as we are," and the burden of that discourse might be read in the "Prayer for Unity." The occasion was deeply interesting, for two years had scarcely elapsed since his, with the other, consecrating hands had been laid on the head of Bishop Wainwright under circumstances which were described by an American writer who was present, in the following words: "Thus auspiciously does Bishop Potter commence his episcopate as the successor of the lamented Bishop Wainwright, with such a gathering of Bishops and Clergy, with one worthy representative of our mother Church of England again entwining the strands of the Apostolic succession in the two Churches, and that, too, by the same hands which were so welcome in the same capacity at the occasion of Bishop Wainwright's consecration."

And this desire to strengthen the "strands of the Apostolic succession" which united the sister Churches of America to the mother Church of England, was conspicuous in the acts of the Canadian Primate. For example, on the 25th March, 1862, being the festival of the Annunciation, when the Right Reverend F. T. Lewis was consecrated at Kingston, as the first Bishop of Ontario, the officiating Bishops were five in number, namely the four Canadian Prelates, and the Right Reverend Samuel McCoskey, D.D., Bishop of Michigan. Nine months later, on Sunday the twenty-first June, 1863, when the Right Rev. T. W. Williams, D.D., was consecrated in succession to Bishop Mountain, as the fourth Bishop of Quebec, the Right Reverend John Hopkins, D.D., the late Bishop of Vermont, at that time Primate of the Episcopal Church in the United States, joined the Canadian Prelates in the service, and laid his hand with theirs on the head of the newly elected Bishop of Quebec.

Such acts of fraternal intercourse preceded the independence which the Anglican Church in Canada may be said to have reached when the Earl of Carnarvon, the Secretary of State for the Colonies, declined to advise Her Majesty to issue any more Royal Mandates for the consecration of Canadian Bishops. This waiver on the part of the Crown included the withdrawal by the Crown of all desire to interfere in ecclesiastical matters, while it left the Church to the undisturbed management of her own affairs. No shock accompanied the announcement, for the mother Church removed her supports with such quiet tenderness, that her daughter was scarcely aware of the separation, when she found herself walking alone. But though the fact of such separation must, we think, be allowed, the time is very remote when Canadian churchmen will describe themselves in any other terms than as members of the Church of England. If this condition of independence is beset with many perils, and some loss, it is not wholly free from elements of compensation. In a worldly point of view the Anglican Church in Canada is but poorly dowered, but she is rich in moral treasure, for she enjoys the blessing and the example of her "Mother dear," the true old Church of England. And such patrimonies, if used aright, may prove of inestimable value as she learns the lessons of self-reliance which her new condition will teach. The course of those lessons may include the duty of drawing more closely the chords of sympathy between herself and her sister, the Episcopal Church of the United States, whose settlements so to speak, are only on the other side of the way. Nor should it be forgotten that this sister, though slightly the senior in age, is of the like condition of life. She has passed through the pain of similar trials as well as through the pleasures of similar hopes. Though often abased neither of them have despaired; for in weal and woe, in elation and in disaster, they have kept their hearts loyal towards the Church of their fathers.

It is true that the history of the two Churches, like the history of the two peoples, must be sought for in separate records, for their careers have differed widely one from the other. The elder and more neglected sister was rocked in the cradle of revolution, while the younger and better cared for, was nursed in the lap of Kings; yet both claim, and with equal truth, the heritage of a common ancestry; both confess their belief in "one Holy Catholic and Apostolic Church;" both cherish the same divine order of the ministry; both do the like work in this world, and look forward to the like welcome in the world to come. It was the patient endeavour of the Canadian Metropolitan, if it may be so expressed, to soften the asperities, and to pave the way to a better understanding and a freer intercourse between the two peoples. Hence his plans were made to bring these separated sisters together, to touch the springs of kinship, to awaken slumbering sympathies, and to call home truant affections. In the spirit of heavenly forbearance he seriously urged upon both peoples to obliterate the red line of blood which had been drawn between their American and English ancestors; to forget the past in the present; and by the threefold obligations of faith, hope and charity, to become spiritually one with one another, as well as with Him who is the God and Father of all the families of the earth.

The soft music of Keble's minstrelsy is dear alike to Englishmen and to Americans, and therefore the mythical representatives of Britannia and Columbia, might attune their harps to the same words and say with the saintly author of *The Christian Year*:

> No distance breaks the tie of blood;
> Brothers are brothers evermore;
> Nor wrong, nor wrath of deadliest mood,
> That magic may o'erpower.
> Oft, ere the common source be known,
> The kindred drops will claim their own,
> And throbbing pulses silently
> Make heart towards heart by sympathy.
>
> So is it with true Christian hearts;
> Their mutual share in Jesus' blood
> An everlasting bond imparts
> Of holiest brotherhood;

Oh! might we all our lineage prove,
Give and forgive, do good and love;
By soft endearments in kind strife
Lighten the load of daily life.

There is much need; for not as yet
  Are we in shelter or repose,
The holy house is still beset
  With leaguer of stern foes;
Wild thoughts within, bad men without,
All evil spirits round about,
Are banded in unblest device
To spoil love's earthly paradise.

Then draw we nearer day by day,
  Each to his brethren, all to God;
Let the world take us as she may,
  We must not change our road;
Nor wondering, though in grief, to find
The martyrs foe still keep her mind;
But fix'd to hold Love's banner fast
An by submission win at last.

CHAPTER FIFTH.

Servant of God! thou hast not long to stay;
Soon the weak bonds that hold thee here shall sever;
Then shalt thou gaze upon the perfect day,
And Him thou lovest, for ever and for ever.

          LYRA ANGLICANA.

ON Saturday, the 16th of September, 1865, being the fourth day of the third Triennial Meeting of the Provincial Synod, the Bishop of Ontario moved the following address, which was carried by both Houses, and in the House of Bishops *nemine contradicente*:

To His Grace CHARLES THOMAS, *Archbishop of Canterbury, D.D., Primate of all England, and Metropolitan:*

MAY IT PLEASE YOUR GRACE,

 We, the Bishops, Clergy and Laity of the Province of Canada, in Triennial Synod assembled, desire to represent to Your Grace that in consequence of the recent decision of the Judicial Committee of the Privy Council, in the well known case respecting the Essays and Reviews, and also in the case of the Bishop of Natal and the Bishop of Capetown, the minds of many members of the Church have been unsettled or painfully alarmed, and that doctrines hitherto believed to be Scriptural and undoubtedly held by the members of the Church of England and Ireland, have been adjudicated upon by the Privy Council in such a way as to lead thousands of our brethren to conclude that according to this decision, it is quite compatible with membership in the Church of England to discredit the historical tacts of Holy Scripture and to disbelieve the eternity of future punishment. Moreover, we would express to Your Grace the intense alarm felt by many in Canada lest the tendency of the revival of the active powers of convocation should leave us governed by Canons different from those in force in England and Ireland, and thus cause us to drift into the status of an independent branch of the Catholic Church, a result which we would at this time most solemnly deplore.

In order therefore to comfort the souls of the faithful and re-assure the minds of the wavering members of the Church and to obviate so far as may be the suspicion whereby so many are scandalized, that the Church is a creation of Parliament, we humbly entreat Your Grace, since the assembly of a general Council of the whole Catholic Church is at present impracticable, to convene a National Synod of the Bishops of the Anglican Church at home and abroad, who, attended by one or more of their Presbyters or Laymen learned in Ecclesiastical law as their advisers, may meet together and under the guidance of the Holy Ghost take such counsel, and adopt such measures, as may be best fitted to provide for the present distress in such Synod presided over by Your Grace.

(Signed,) F. MONTREAL,
Metropolitan, President.

(Signed,) JAS. BEAVEN, D.D.,
Prolocutor.

If we are not mistaken, the Bishop of Ontario at the time of his consecration was the most youthful member of his order in the British Dominions. Besides the grand qualifications of youth and learning, Bishop Lewis is said to be a remorseless logician, deeply read in ecclesiastical law, fertile in resource and full of enthusiasm. Moreover he is courageous by nature and aggressive from duty, sanguine by temperament and adventurous from necessity. Being a confident as well as a bold man he is thoroughly inclined to face difficulties in the persons of those who make them. Less ardent men would probably have hesitated before committing themselves to a resolution whose success included a gathering in one great National Synod of Bishops, Presbyters and Laymen, the representatives of the Anglican Church, in almost every part of the habitable globe.

Happily the Primate of England was by no means disinclined to sympathize with the Bishop of Ontario, or to take the necessary steps for meeting the duty which the address of the Canadian Synod laid upon him. The following letter from his Grace on the subject will be read with interest:

To the Bishops, Clergy and Laity of the Province of Canada, lately assembled in their Triennial Synod.

ADDINGTON PARK.

MY RIGHT REV., REV. AND DEAR BRETHREN,

I have duly received the Address forwarded to me by your Metropolitan, from the late Triennial Provincial Synod of the Province of Canada, requesting me to convene a Synod of the Bishops of the Anglican Church, both at home and abroad, in order that they may meet together, and under the guidance of the Holy Ghost, take such counsel, and adopt such measures as may be best fitted to provide for the present distress.

I can well understand your surprise and alarm at the recent decisions of the Judicial Committee of the Privy Council, in grave matters bearing upon the doctrine and discipline of our Church, and I can comprehend your anxiety, lest the recent revival of action in the two Provincial Convocations of Canterbury and York, should lead to the disturbance of those relations which have hitherto subsisted between the different branches of the Anglican Church.

The meeting of such a Synod as you propose is not by any means foreign to my own feelings, and I think it might tend to prevent those inconveniences the possibility of which you anticipate. I cannot however take any step in so grave a matter, without consulting my Episcopal Brethren in both Branches of the United Church of England and Ireland, as well as those in the different Colonies, dependencies of the British Empire.

I remain,
Your faithful and affectionable Friend and Brother in Christ,

C. T. CANTUAR,
Primate of all England.

December, 1865.

After due consideration the Archbishop issued the requisite mandate, and subsequently gave his earnest attention to the object for which that mandate was made by presiding at the Lambeth Conference.

As the address which gave rise to the Conference emanated from the Ecclesiastical Province of Canada, it followed naturally that the Metropolitan of that Province should be expected to take a prominent part in the proceedings of that Conference, nor was that Most Reverend Prelate the man to flinch from the responsibility of his vote, much less to decline any labour to which that vote gave rise. No doubt the novelty of the occasion added much to their difficulties, who were required to manage the Conference and determine what questions should be avoided and what discussed; for it was especially desirable that a great Convocation gathered for the furtherance of unity should not be disturbed by offences against charity.

It is no part of our plan to criticize the merits of that grand assembly any more than it is a part of our duty to hazard an opinion on the character of the benefits which may be expected to flow from it. That it was not without present advantages has been generally conceded and is commonly believed. Nevertheless those advantages were regarded as of an evanescent character, when compared with the greater and more lasting blessings which that unprecedented assembly may be expected to inaugurate. But even should it have been nothing more than a majestic ceremonial for "casting bread upon the waters," it was at all events such an one as fully justifies the belief that it will bear fruit after many days; but whatever the result may be, the germ of that result must be sought for in the zeal of a Canadian Bishop and in the action of the Canadian Church.

The Archbishop of Canterbury died in the month after the death of the Metropolitan of Canada. We shall presently refer to the opinion of the latter on the Lambeth Conference. In this place it may be interesting to note what the former thought of it. The following letter addressed to the Bishop of Illinois is extracted from a charge lately delivered by that Prelate to his clergy. The Bishop of Illinois thus prefaces the letter: "With some misgiving in yielding to the temptation, I venture to add a portion of a letter from that best of men, to whose wisdom, love and firmness the success of the meeting was eminently due."

ADDINGTON PARK.

DEAR BISHOP OF ILLINOIS,

May you have a safe voyage across the Atlantic, and may you find all in your Diocese at peace, and abounding in the fruits of the Spirit. For myself, I shall always look back on the Conference as an important era in my life and Arch-Episcopate. I trust that it has tended to bind the different branches of the Church in our Anglican Communion more closely together in the bonds of brotherly love. The Encyclical, as I have heard from good authority, is considered a very serious matter by Roman Catholics—English and Foreign; and some of them have said that the Church of Rome has never received such a blow since the Reformation. Then, the vehemence with which the Infidel press has attacked the Conference plainly shows what importance they attach to the movement. Altogether, I trust, we may thank God, and take courage.

I must not conclude without thanking you for the important aid which you rendered to the cause of the Congress throughout. But for you, in February, I certainly should not have had the courage to invite our Brethren from the United States.

I am deeply thankful that I was permitted to do so, and it will be long before the pleasing recollections of my intercourse with so many of them can fade from my memory.

Believe me, dear Bishop of Illinois,

Your faithful and affectionate Friend and Brother,

C. T. CANTUAR.

December 27th, 1867.

Honour generally includes labour as well as responsibility, and it is possible that the duties which success imposed pressed heavily on the mind of the Canadian Metropolitan, especially as His Lordship's health had previously been in an unsatisfactory state. At all events, it is certain that some, who welcomed him on his return to Canada, remarked that he did not look as well as they hoped he would have done after an interval of residence, if not of rest, in his native land. Prolonged absence from his diocese had been attendant with a certain accumulation of work, which a Bishop only could perform, and therefore the Metropolitan lost no time in "setting in order things that were wanting."

On Tuesday, the 16th of June, 1868, the annual meeting of the Diocesan Synod took place at Montreal. The Metropolitan preached, and on the same day delivered an address which was unusually interesting, for it sparkled with reflections freshly caught from the life and work of the Church at home. In the course of his address, His Lordship referred to the proceedings of the Lambeth Conference in the following suggestive and encouraging words:

Well, we met, and notwithstanding the doubts of the timid and the sneers of the scornful, though every thing may not have been done that some eager, ardent spirits hoped or expected, though we had no constituted legal character, and never for an instant affected to claim it; yet I unhesitatingly assert that if those seventy-six Archbishops and Bishops, holding office in the Church of Christ, and representing the Anglo-Catholic branch of that Church, having come together at the Archbishop's invitation—every particular Province or portion of that Church, in every quarter of the world, having one or more representatives in that august assembly; there being 23 from England and Ireland; 6 from Scotland; 28 Colonial; and 19 from the United States; some having travelled ten and twelve thousand miles in order to attend,—if we have done nothing more than given visible testimony to our oneness in faith and discipline by our united acts of public worship, and promulgating that solemn address to the faithful, contained in the "Encyclical Letter," which was so carefully drawn up and signed by all present,—then I unhesitatingly assert, that we have done the most important act connected with the maintenance of the true faith, as we have received it, and the establishment of the Church of Christ as a living witness for the truth, that has been accomplished for many hundreds of years.

The Metropolitan knew not that he was addressing the clergy and laity of his diocese for the last time. Like the beloved Apostle, he had "no new commandment to give," for his last, like his first words were beauty laden with lessons of forbearance and charity, of peace and unity. Almost immediately after the close of the Diocesan Synod, he visited the Eastern Townships and attended the annual Convocation of the University of Bishops College, Lennoxville. The deep interest which he had always taken in the welfare of that important educational institution, became increasingly conspicuous and was never more apparent than on the occasion on which he spoke within its walls for the last time. His Lordship had probably caught the geniality and animation of the Rev. Canon Balch, who preceded him, for he spoke with a heartiness that was all aglow with congratulation and encouragement. The friends of the University were pleasantly affected and not without cause. The vision which rose before them seemed to be bright with the reflection of a "good time coming," for from the Chancellor to the least distinguished member of that University, all were moved with the same desire to look cheerfully at their responsibilities and resolutely at their duties, and to discharge both with honest and willing minds. Afterwards His Lordship made a Confirmation tour through the Deanery of St. Andrews, and, as we learn from the published sermon of his Chaplain, the Rev. Canon Loosemore, spoke to the candidates who were presented to him for the "laying on of hands," with unwonted earnestness and fervour, as if his thoughts had even then ceased to be of the earth, and were the reflections of the "better land," to which he was fast hastening.

Six days before the time appointed for the meeting of the Provincial Synod, the Metropolitan returned to Montreal, and began to take measures for the meeting at which it was his duty to preside. But his work was done, a sense of oppressive weariness overtook him, attended with a feeling of langour and a desire for rest. The disease to which he was prone no longer yielded to the influence of medicine, and the doctors looked anxiously at one another. His wife, who had been every thing to him, stood nervously on the threshold of widowhood, and the few chosen friends by whom he was attended whispered their fears as if the days of mourning were come. But while many were watching anxiously the ebb of his retreating life, he was only concerned about the duty he could no longer discharge. Like Wolfe, when dying on the plains of Abraham, or like Nelson, in the Bay of Trafalgar, the sense of duty triumphed over death, for in the midst of suffering and weakness, when clouds and darkness were gathering about him, his enquiry was "How is the Synod getting on."

The school-room in which that Synod was assembled to work, was separated only by a partition wall from the house in which he, who had called it together, was lying down to die. On one side of that wall, delegates from every part of Canada were gathered together to take counsel about "Christ's Church Militant here upon earth." On the other side of that wall, in the modest house built for the Parish Schoolmaster, he who had called those delegates together, the heir presumptive of Great Fulford, and the Metropolitan of Canada, was quietly passing to the Church triumphant in heaven.

> "His work was done, and like a warrior olden,
> The hard fight o'er, he laid his armour down,
> And passed, all silent, through the portal golden,
> Where gleams the victor's crown."

As we read what did take place at that Synod, we ask ourselves in vain, what more the Metropolitan would have said on the general subject of the Lambeth Conference as well as on the especial subject of ritual, which at his suggestion had been remitted by his Diocesan to the Provincial Synod for consideration. But in the absence of such knowledge, the earnest observations made by him on the latter subject to the Synod of his diocese, are worthy of the most thoughtful study.

If there are, said His Lordship, excesses on the part of the so-called ritualists, there are undeniably many sad deficiencies in the other extreme. The ritual of the Church of England, if faithfully observed, is fully capable, whether adapted to the service of the noblest cathedral or minster, or to the humblest country church, of satisfying the wants and cravings of all her faithful children without transgressing what, Sir Robert Phillimore remarks, are the only orders given in the New Testament respecting ritual, and they are of the most general kind, such as the directions of St. Paul to the Corinthians—"Let all things be done to edification." "Let all things be done decently and in order." And at the close of his judgment he says: The basis of the religious establishment in this realm was, I am satisfied, intended by the constitution and the law to be broad and not narrow." Within its walls there is room for those whose devotion is so supported by simple faith and fervent piety, that they desire no aid from external ceremony or ornament, and who think that these things degrade and obscure religion. And for those who think with Burke, that religion should be performed, as all public solemn acts are performed, in buildings, in music, in decorations, in speech, in the dignity of persons, according to the customs of mankind taught by their nature, that is with modest splendour and unassuming pomp; who sympathize with Milton the poet, rather than with Milton the puritan, and says that these accessories of religious rites—

'Dissolve them into ecstacies,
And bring all heaven before their eyes.'

St. Chrysostom and St. Augustine represented different schools of religious thought; the Primitive Church held them both. Bishop Tagner and Archbishop Leighton differed as to ceremonial observances, but they prayed for the good estate of the same Catholic Church; they held the same faith "In unity of spirit, in the bond of peace and in righteousness of life;" and the English Church contained them both.

And now I will end this rather lengthened address by quoting a short passage at the close of the preface to a recent work, entitled, "Studies in the Gospels," by the Archbishop of Dublin, already so well known to you from his excellent works on the parables and miracles of our Lord. "For my labours," he says, "I shall be abundantly repaid if now, when so many controversies are drawing away the Christian student from the rich and quiet pastures of scripture to other fields, not perhaps barren, but which can yield no such nourishment as these do, I shall have contributed aught to detain any among them. May we all, amidst the labours and excitement of the battle of life, find time to be much in those rich and quiet pastures; and may the food there gathered by God's grace so assimilate with our natures as to produce in us its own spirit of love, which is, after all, "the end of the commandment," and "the fulfilling of the law."

Apart from the circumstances under which the address was delivered, the words themselves were weighty words, and deserved more respect than they appeared to receive from some of the members of the Provincial Synod who discussed the subject. Let such gentlemen, clerical or lay, who so far forgot the purpose for which they were assembled as to degrade the occasion into one for facetious levity and unseemly jokes, seriously say whether a subject, the investigation of which had been deemed of sufficient moment to justify the issue of a Royal Commission, was not of sufficient moment to be approached without merriment, and discussed without sneers. Men do not commonly accept the standard of their neighbour's prejudice as their rule of law, either in sacred or in secular matters. They look to ecclesiastical judges to interpret the laws of the church just as they do to civil judges to interpret the laws of the state. Nor were thoughtful churchmen unmindful of the law, as it had lately been laid down by Sir Robert Phillimore in his exhaustive judgment when among other things that eminent Jurist said : " The basis of the religious establishment in this realm was, I am satisfied, intended by the constitution and the law to be broad and not narrow."

Would it not become those who have been especially chosen to promote the peace, welfare and good government of the newly constituted branch of the Anglican Church in Canada to season their correction of the mother Church with caution, lest in their zeal they should reverse the design of her constitution by making that narrow which was intended to be broad? A national church, like a national government, should represent the nation. It should be sufficiently broad to embrace within its influence, all whom infidelity and unbelief have not excluded or expelled. Parties have always and probably will always exist within the church as well as within the state, and though we may choose to consider the fact an inconvenience, it may nevertheless be for our moral and intellectual health that it is so. Our human nature is made up of many parts and crossed with many qualities, for diversity and not uniformity may be looked upon as the condition of that nature. The wisdom of the Church seems to take cognizance of this condition and adapt its laws thereto. Feeling and poetry, for example, a passion for music, or a taste for art, are frequently observed to be among the controlling influences which move individuals. Such influences, be it remembered, are equally His gifts who bestows the ability to reason, or the capacity to reflect. If then it be the office of religion to cleanse and purify our whole nature, it may also be the office of religion to do so by every means which charity approves, so long as such means are not repugnant to the divine law.

Therefore, wherever such means minister to holy and religious ends, such for example as the practice of charity, the love of purity, and the observance of truth, they are at least worthy of the thoughtful consideration of all, and especially of those who honestly and fervently strive to cleanse every sense, every feeling and every passion of the heart; for they are the pure in heart who shall see God. Let us not miss what is edifying in order that we may avoid what is hurtful, for religion not only sanctifies common things, but has some general directions on the order of divine service, and some especial ones on the reverence due to sacred places. "The house of the Lord and the offices thereof" create, in the minds of the Christian, feelings akin to those which they excited in the heart of the Jew. Reverence for God's sanctuary prompts men to add beauty to use. The adornment of our Christian temples is, as it should be, regarded as a reasonable service, even though such service, like the broken box of spikenard, be made at a cost and sacrifice of much "that might have been given to the poor." Members of the Anglican Church in various ways should be, and are, required to mark the progress of the Christian year. At Christmas time, during our festival of "Peace and good will," we deck "our Cathedral roofs" with verdure, and array the walls of our temples with "living green." To this end we gather tribute from "the fir tree, the pine tree and the box together." At

Easter and Whitsuntide we may scatter flowers upon our altars and beautify our Churches with lilies, not unlike those which the author of our faith commanded His disciples to consider. In like manner it is in harmony with his injunctions who has told us to "worship the Lord in the beauty of holiness," that we should not overlook what is seemly in appearance as well as what is convenient in design. Almost all denominations of Christians, for example, have trained officers to lead their service of praise, and whether such officers be called, "precentors" or "parish clerks," "choir men" or "choir boys," it is as decent as it is usual to mark their office by clothing them in the livery of the sanctuary, no matter whether such dress be a black gown or a linen ephod. It is enough that the dress is suited to the place and to the duty which those who wear it are called upon to perform. Such observances are among the outward decencies of worship, and have nothing whatever to do with doctrinal errors or with the offences of ritual.

Ritualism, like Rationalism, is abominable when, after the manner of Balaam, it seeks to corrupt our faith, and not after the example of David, to elevate our worship. It is abominable when it seeks to weaken the testimony of Holy Scripture, and to destroy the value of Church history. It is abominable when it makes light of the noblest incidents of English story and the noblest acts of English worthies. It is abominable when it blots with calumny the best pages of our national literature and the brightest portions of our national life. It is abominable when it dishonours the memory of our martyrs and discredits the testimony of our confessors, when it sneers at their protest against error, and regards as of little worth the name of "Protestant," which, as devout Catholics, they won from those whose usurpations they protested against and whose errors they exposed. These, and such as these, are they whom churchmen have to fear and to avoid, no matter whether they approach in the livery of the ritualist or in the nakedness of the rationalist.

In their successive sessions the Provincial Synod, if we may be allowed to speak its praise, has done well to scratch as counterfeit the excesses of both parties, and to denounce, with a view to their avoidance, what is actually as well as what is symbolically corrupt. But in our jealousy for what is right and true, it may be wise to remember that there is room within the limits of our Prayer Books for a diversity of opinion while there is no room for unbelief. On matters indifferent we can tolerate, though we are not required to admire, the ecclesiastical vagaries which appear to beset men of extreme views. It is not difficult, for example, to be patient towards one school of teachers of earnest endeavour and unquestionable piety, who, for reasons of their own, appear to think that there is a good deal of merit in performing divine service in dresses of strongly contrasted colours. We can also tolerate, though we cannot understand, another school of teachers, who deem it to be equally commendable to array their altars in what may be called memorial and effective clothing. The proceeding, in both cases, is partially unintelligible and wholly sectarian. The difference seems to be that the ministers of one party are distinguishable by the symbolic colours in which they clothe themselves, and the ministers of the other party are distinguishable by the symbolic colours in which they clothe their altars.

There may be, perhaps there is, a corresponding difference in the teaching of the two parties. The former, as it seems to us, is dangerously inclined to belittle the grace, and to discredit the blessings, of the sacraments by ceaseless exhortations to their hearers to guard against what they call a "sacramental religion," while the latter, being possessed of a different reason for alarm, insist that it is only by a "sacramental religion" that the spiritual life can either be received or continued in the soul. Though both parties cannot be equally right, they may be equally in earnest, while, as a matter of fact, they must be equally sectarian. It is probable that in Canada at least, the teaching of such extremists, if left to themselves, would counteract one another, and in time would approximate towards the opinions of the larger, safer, and more reasonable mass which constitutes the great body of the church. Old-fashioned members of the Anglican communion have little relish for theological extravagance and none for ecclesiastical eccentricity, no matter whether it manifests itself in sectarian preaching or in sectarian postures. Unfortunately the smaller sects within the Church, by the force of zeal rather than by the force of truth, exert influences beyond the spheres they are supposed to control. The decent and comely order of divine worship has, in this way, very unnecessarily become mixed up with what is variable in colour or whimsical in gesture, while in some places it is associated with what is questionable in doctrine and contradictory in practice. It thus happens that some things that are manifestly desirable and would tend to edification, are laid aside as hurtful or postponed as inexpedient, because nervous or narrow-minded people very naturally, though very illogically, regard all changes as developments of erroneous dogma or repudiated usages.

The moderation of the late Metropolitan was known to and acknowledged by all. No character was more offensive and obnoxious to him than the theological partizan. Being thoroughly sincere he delighted in sincerity, for he knew that where there is sincerity there will there be charity. The religious partizan was his dread, as it is the dread of all sincere Christians. Let us not lightly part with the grace of moderation, which is the especial heritage of the Anglican Church. Let us not surrender our reason to our fears, or at the bidding of fanaticism pay a cowardly tribute to clamour; for should the control of our Synods, or the government of our Church, fall into the hands of sectarian or narrow-minded rulers, of men who will fight about a posture or fume about a robe, the day may arrive when it will be said of us as it is unfortunately, but we trust erroneously, said of the Anglican Church in Ireland, that the "mission of the Protestant Church is a failure."

The Metropolitan was a man of large and generous views. Like Dr. Tait, the present Archbishop of Canterbury, he desired to encourage zealous and hard-working men in his diocese, no matter to what especial party they belonged. Unlike the Archbishop the Canadian Primate could scarcely be said to cheer any one on his way, for he seemed to have an old-fashioned disinclination to praise a man for doing his duty. Moreover he was reserved by nature and undemonstrative by habit and therefore the form of his encouragement was neither particularly warm, nor particularly genial. Nevertheless, and as if to illustrate the rule by the exception, it is recorded that on occasion and under pressure his Lordship could be incautious as well as encouraging. For example, when Mr. Wood, the incumbent of the Free Church of St. John the Evangelist, Montreal, was violently assailed in the Diocesan Synod, the English character and college habit of the Bishop immediately showed itself, as irrespective of the merits of the case he generously took the weaker side, and spoke of Mr. Wood in language of unusual compliment, giving the Synod to understand that he could befriend a zealous clergyman, and that he would do so, if he thought him unfairly beset with numbers.

But it was contrary to his practice either to praise or to blame. The only occasion we can recall on which he publicly did the former, was in the case we have mentioned, and that was evidently unpremeditated. The only occasion in like manner, of which he had any recollection of his doing the latter, was in his well known controversy with Archdeacon Hellmuth, and that was evidently ill-considered. No reasonable doubt existed that the Archdeacon's Islington speech was open to criticism as a matter of taste, as well as to question as a matter of fact. In justice therefore to his own order, which had fallen under the Archdeacon's animadversion, as well as to the clergy of his ecclesiastical province, who had generally been assailed, the Metropolitan, as we think, very properly determined to break silence and administer a censure. But to praise or to blame, as we have said, were practices equally foreign to his experience. When he indulged in the former with respect to Mr. Wood, or in the latter with respect to Archdeacon

Hellmuth, he displayed a warmth contrary to his habit. In resisting, what he deemed to be unfair, and in rebuking what he deemed to be unfounded, he exhibited the heat of an undergraduate rather than the serenity of a moderator. On both occasions he permitted himself, as we infer, to be led by his feelings to the detriment of his judgment, and we may add to the injury of his cause. In fact the warmth of the interference weakened the value of it. Mr. Wood's tendency, as we have been informed, is to depreciate his own and to speak generously of his neighbour's merits, and therefore he would scarcely have welcomed compliments paid to him at the expense of his clerical brethren, who to the best of their judgment were engaged in work similar to his own. In like manner, the reproof, which Archdeacon Hellmuth had taken some pains to deserve, went somewhat wide of the mark, because it had been indiscreetly feathered with feeling and embarrassed with side issues that were foreign to, and diverted attention from, the cause of offence. The Metropolitan's reputation for prudence suffered from the unguarded way in which a special charge in one instance was answered by a general compliment, and in the other by a general accusation. This effort to extend his position beyond the reach of his supports was in the last degree incautious, and in the instances under review occasioned the loss of many advantages he might otherwise have gained.

These exceptions impaired but they did not destroy the character for wisdom which the Metropolitan enjoyed and by which he will be remembered. We have already referred to the moderation of his government and to his determination to administer the affairs of his diocese as the ruler of a church, which permits of much latitude of opinion, and not as the leader of a sect whose tenets are absolutely clasped within the bands of a rigid fanaticism. No doubt the Metropolitan had clearly defined opinions on the questions of the day, for on fitting occasions he took no pains to conceal them; but he was too conscientious a ruler to substitute his individual opinion for the law of the church, and too acute a jurist not to be aware that even a law may admit of a liberal, and comprehensive, as well as of an exact and technical interpretation. Civil and religious freedom were no mere phrases with him, and therefore he was incapable of showing by his practice that such phrases meant the liberty to think in civil matters only as he thought, or act in religious matters only as he acted.

These examples must be looked upon as exceptional. We shall select one illustration of his judicial conduct that will better illustrate the equity of his judgment and the evenness of his mental balance. In the matter of the Bishop of Huron's objections to what was called "the theological teaching" of Trinity College, Toronto, certain questions were put by the Council of that University to the Bishops of the Province of Canada. The answers given by their Lordships were interesting and instructive, and are especially worthy of the regard of all who desire to approach the solution of the difficulty in a fair and reasonable frame of mind. The answers, we may observe in passing, are characteristic of their authors, and we may add of the races from which those authors derive. Those, for example, of the Bishops of Huron and Ontario, though directly opposed to one another, have a natural warmth and raciness about them, as if mental gymnastics were exhialrating to the Milesian temperaments of both, and especially of one, of those Right Reverend Prelates. The Metropolitan and the Bishop of Quebec, on the contrary, were phlegmatic Englishmen, and their answers are only calm and dispassionate criticisms, well calculated by their judicial analysis and even tone to quiet prejudice and silence opponents. Indeed, the case was so fairly and so broadly put that the public mind was set at rest, and the public confidence continued in the teaching of an institution that had evidently been assailed with more zeal than exactness, and altogether with more warmth than the occasion warranted or excused.

On the ninth of September, 1868, in obedience to the summons of the Metropolitan, the Triennial Meeting of the Provincial Synod took place. The usual service was held in the Cathedral, where the Holy Communion was celebrated. The Right Reverend R. Mackray, D.D., the Bishop of Rupert's land preached. The services, as well as the informal meeting of the Delegates that followed, were in the highest degree affecting. Some conversation took place at the latter on the peculiar and trying circumstances in which the Synod found itself, as well as on the course it would be advisable to pursue. Then an adjournment to the following day was agreed upon, but before the motion was put, the Right Reverend A. N. Bethune, D.D, the Bishop of Toronto, offered up a prayer " to the Father of mercies and the God of all comfort," that he would give strength and succour to His servant, the Metropolitan of Canada, who was then " sick unto death," and no doubt there were many there present who in the words of the office for the Communion of the sick devoutly commended their brother and spiritual father into the hands of a faithful Creator. The Synod then separated. When it again assembled on the following day, the Metropolitical See was vacant, for the soul of the Primate being, so to speak, pillowed on the prayers of the faithful, had ascended with the evening sacrifice to God. On the ninth of September, 1868, at twenty minutes past six o'clock, literally at the "fall of eve," the blessed words ADESTE FIDELES were, it may have been, by holy voices spoken, for the soul of the pilgrim, who in weakness and suffering had been struggling on the "thorn road," was borne beyond the brightness of the sun, and amidst the joy of angels, lodged in the light of God.

Under such circumstances, and with such human surroundings, the last Bishop appointed by the Crown for the Anglican Church in Canada surrendered his sacred trust. The emblems of his office and ministry, the mitre and the crozier, the scallop shell and the staff, were laid aside, and from the very centre of duty, encircled by the congregated representatives of his Province, the Primate of Canada entered the presence chamber of the King of Kings.

> Two hands upon the breast,
>   And labour's done;
> Two pale feet crossed in rest,
>   The race is won;
> Two eyes with coin weights shut,
>   And all tears cease;
> Two lips where grief is mute,
>   And all is peace!

Three days afterwards, on the twelfth of September, the funeral took place, and we may add in strict accordance with his Lordship's quiet and unostentatious character. The plate on his metal coffin, which was shaped like a mitre, bore the following simple inscription:

FRANCIS FULFORD, D.D.,

LORD BISHOP OF MONTREAL AND METROPOLITAN OF CANADA,

Born 3rd of June, 1803.

Died 9th September, 1868.

But while the funeral arrangements were conspicuous for their simplicity, they were accompanied with expressions of public sorrow that were almost universal. Every class of society was seen amongst those who followed his hearse, and stood by his grave. Officers of the Civil and Military departments were there, together with the Provosts of Universities, and the members of the learned professions. Clergymen from every part of Canada, and ministers of various Christian denominations were there, together with some of the Jewish persuasion. The Clerical and Lay Delegates in attendance at the Provincial Synod were there, including several* Presbyters, who had received their orders with the imposition of his hands, and who in some instances stood hard by the place where on trussel pedestals and in the view of that great congregation the first Metropolitan of Canada slept his last sleep. Tearful eyes no

---

* For list of persons ordained to the sacred ministry by the Right Rev. Francis Fulford, D.D., see Appendix to this sketch, page 130.

doubt were there, and sad hearts too. Hearts that revered their Bishop and loved their Church,—hearts that were troubled about many things, and especially whether a successor of equal wisdom and moderation would be found to wear the mantle and take the place which the poor tenant of that coffin had filled so well. Meanwhile the grand organ throbbed like muffled music, and with subtle power seemed to articulate the general grief. When it sank into silence, the voice of the Very Reverend Dean Bethune, the friend and commissary of the deceased Prelate, in accents weakened alike with age and grief, slowly repeated the words of the affecting office for the burial of the dead. The Dean was followed by the Venerable Archdeacon Leach, in like manner the dear friend of the Metropolitan, who read the appointed lesson taken from the fifteenth chapter of the first epistle to the Corinthians. Those sublime words of challenge and victory over death and the grave had scarcely been uttered, when for the last time the Metropolitan passed out of the Cathedral, which he had helped to build, to the Cemetery of Mount Royal, which he had consecrated and set apart for the burial of the dead. The tolling of the great bell of the Anglican Cathedral was answered by the tolling of the great bell of the Roman Catholic Church of Notre-Dame, for the authorities of the latter, like their protestant fellow subjects, paid spontaneous tribute to the worth and memory of Bishop Fulford, and hence many gentlemen of French descent were noticed in the procession which followed his remains to the grave. That grave was at length reached. The voice of the Dean was again heard in the solemn words "we commit his body to the ground," and then the crumbled earth fell upon the coffin, and dust and ashes welcomed their kindred. The peaceful benediction pronounced by the Reverend Canon Bond followed the concluding prayer, and then the grave was closed. When all was over and men whispered one with another as the sextons plied their calling, some remarked, and perhaps all remembered, that that day was an important anniversary in the history of the Anglican Church in Canada, for it was on the twelfth of September, 1836, that the Right Rev. G. J. Mountain, the first Prelate of that Church, who, as the suffragan of the Bishop of Quebec, bore the title of Bishop of Montreal, arrived in his diocese; and it was on that day eighteen years, on the twelfth of September, 1850, that the first Bishop of the diocese of Montreal and the first Metropolitan of Canada, arrived in the city; and now, on the twelfth of September, 1868, the mortal remains of him who had received both commissions, and discharged the duties of both offices, who had won the highest honours in, and dispensed the fullest powers of the Canadian Church, were placed in the quiet earth, there to rest until angel voices shall say to all who sleep in Jesus:

"AWAKE AND SING YE THAT DWELL IN DUST."

APPENDIX.

List of persons admitted to Holy Orders by the Most REVEREND FRANCIS FULFORD, D.D.

Names.	Year of Ordination.	Names.	Year of Ordination.
† Abbott, C. P.	1859	† Lancaster, C. H.	1864
* Allan, John	1859	† Lewis, P. P.	1860
Allnatt, F. J. B.	1865	* Lindsay, Robert	1851
Anderson, William	1859	† Lindsay, David	1851
† Babin, Jeremie	1864	* Lockhart, A. D.	1851
Birtch, R. S.	1852	† McLeod, Jas. A.	1853
† Borthwick, J. D.	1864	† Merrick, Joseph	1862
* Bousall, Thomas	1858	† Montgomery, H.	1854
† Brown, W. R.	1866	† Morris, J. A.	1852
Burgess, H. F.	1868	† Mussen, T. W.	1855
† Burt, Frederick	1853	* Nesbitt, A. C.	1864
Carden, R. A.	1852	* O'Grady, G. De C.	1851
† Codd, Francis	1860	† Parker, G. H.	1863
* Constantine, J.	1852	Prime, Augustus	1868
† Curran, W. B.	1861	† Reade, John	1864
† Daniel, C. A.	1865	† Robinson, G. C.	1865
† Dart, W. J.	1867	† Rollit, John	1866
† Davidson, J.	1856	Roy, Edward	1868
† Davidson, J. B.	1861	† Scarth, A. C.	1857
† Davidson, J. C.	1854	† Seaborn, W. M.	1861
De Moulpied, J.	1856	† Seaman, John	1863
* Du Vernet, Edward	1852	† Smith, John	1862
† Fessenden, E. G.	1865	* Smith, P. W.	1866
† Fortin, A. L.	1864	* Stephenson, R. L.	1851
† Fortin, Octave	1865	† Sykes, J. S.	1854
† Fyles, T. W.	1862	† Taylor, A. C.	1862
† Godden, John	1854	† Thorndike, C. F.	1866
† Godden, Thomas	1863	† Wetherall, C. A.	1854
† Gribble, John	1856	† Williams, S. P.	1854
* Griffin, Joseph	1852	Wilson, Frederick	1853
Jones, Septimus	1854	* Wood, Edmund	1861
Judd, F. E.	1852	Wright, William	1864
† Kaapcke, C. J.	1865		

* Those marked thus received Priest's orders only.
† Those marked thus received Deacon's and Priest's orders.
Those not indicated by a special mark received Deacon's orders only.
The year indicates the period when the ordinations took place. In cases where clergymen received both orders, the time at which Deacon's orders was given is only noted.

The Right Reverend
George J. Mountain, D.D., D.C.L.,
Third Bishop of Quebec.

The view of religion which commended itself to his mind was the practical application of the Gospel of our Lord Jesus Christ to the wants of men; and the best method of doing this was, in his opinion, a simple and faithful adherence to the principles and rules of the Prayer Book. I never met with a more sincere Christian, or one who had less of the spirit of party. I never met with a man whose religious system seemed to be more completely within the four corners of the Book of Common Prayer. For religious speculation he had little taste —for religious eccentricities he had an utter abhorrence; but if there was any deed to be done, any work of mercy to be performed, either for the bodies or the souls of men, then his whole heart was engaged. To go about doing good was the only employment that he thoroughly and unreservedly loved."
—DEAN GOODWIN'S IMPRESSIONS OF BISHOP MACKENZIE.

THE RIGHT REVEREND
GEORGE J. MOUNTAIN, D.D., D.C.L.,

THIRD BISHOP OF QUEBEC.

CHAPTER FIRST.

I'll spurn the hated Bourbon's realm, his blood stain'd floreal-lis,
And seek beneath a foreign flag a home where thought is free.

I'll leave the smiling fields of France; abjure her King and cause;
My fealty henceforth shall be his, whose banner is the Lord's.

Welcome the forest and the cave; welcome the ocean's foam;
Welcome the martyr's stake and grave; but not the faith of Rome.

Though earth may yield no place of rest, my faith can pierce the sky,
In heaven above my witness is, my record is on high!

For Thee, O Lord, I'll bear my cross; for Thee endure the shame;
In weal and woe, midst hate and scorn, I'll bless Thy holy name.

But help me in my weakness, Lord, to keep my conscience pure;
To count all worldly loss a gain; to suffer and endure.

The Lay of the Huguenot.—ERASMUS OLDSTYLE.

COULD Louis the Fourteenth have foreseen the national reverses that followed, and, in the opinion of some historians, were chiefly occasioned by the revocation of the Edict of Nantes, he would scarcely have authorized that cruel and impolitic measure. Patriotism would have rebuked bigotry and silenced evil counsellors, for though he delighted to style himself the "eldest son of the Church," he was too worldly a monarch and too great a King to enrich a rival power at the expense of his own people. But acuteness, like humanity, not unfrequently pay tribute to fanaticism. Religion in his practice was a policy and not a conviction, and hence he had little respect for the faith, and none for the scruples of his subjects. The sufferings and the sacrifices which those subjects underwent in resisting his decrees were probably matters of speculative surprize to Louis, who knew little of the power and nothing of the rights of conscience.

The apparent contumacy of his protestant subjects at length exasperated the arrogant king. By wounding his pride they excited his vengeance; but to gratify the latter without stint it was necessary to submit to Rome without reserve. Therefore Louis the Fourteenth accepted the policy of Richelieu, as interpreted by Mazarin, and remorselessly carried out by Ann of Austria. He trampled his protestant subjects in the dust, and by setting at naught the religious liberty of which Henry the Fourth had laid the foundation, he did much to destroy what was left of the independence of the Gallican Church. Thus, to some extent, were brought about the reverses that overtook France, as well as the miseries that not only humiliated, but well nigh overthrew, the house of Bourbon. For after this manner Massillon spoke, when preaching before the King, in the first years of the eighteenth century: " God has given us, our children, our husbands, our brothers and our friends unto the sword of our enemies. He has breathed upon our armies a spirit of terror and panic, and He has baffled all our hopes."

The immediate result of the effort to affront every French Protestant was to create discontent and to provoke resistance, to impoverish and render disaffected large masses of the population, and negatively as well as positively to deplete the strength of France. But the direct, though more remote consequence, was not only to increase the number, and augment the resources of her enemies, but to add the element of cruelty to the wrongs by which enemies were moved ; thus it was that the aversions and hatreds as well as the culture and skill which accompanied the Huguenots to other lands, increased the moral as well as the economical wealth of those lands, and contributed one of the strongest elements to those forces that were rapidly gathering to challenge the power of the French king and to resist the assumptions of the Roman See. The record of disasters, which commenced shortly after the event we have mentioned, received frightful additions before the close of Louis' reign only to grow larger in the reign of his successor, when the vanquished armies of France were withdrawn from the outposts, to do duty at the seat of empire. Thus, in the East and in the West, the soldiers of that fair land were routed by the forces of their indomitable rival, till at length, in one of those battles which history has stamped as "decisive," the Latin race, through its representative, the king of France, surrendered, with the citadel of Quebec, half a continent and sixty-five thousand French subjects to the sovereignty of the King of England. In connection with the conquest of Canada, and as one of the minor historical incidents that owe their existence to the revocation of the Edict of Nantes, we may observe that, in establishing the church of the new rulers in the newly acquired country, a descendant of one of those Huguenots whom Louis the Fourteenth had driven from France, was consecrated as the first Anglican Bishop of the province which Louis the Fifteenth surrendered to England.

Of the hosts of Protestants who were ejected or who escaped from France—differently estimated from two hundred and fifty to ten hundred thousand persons—at least fifty thousand, it has been computed, sought and found sanctuary in England. The latter included persons of all estates and conditions; men of leisure and education were among the refugees, as well as manufacturers and traders, cultivators and craftsmen, weavers and artizans. In the first mentioned class was a Monsieur Jacob de Montaigne, who possibly owned a portion of the land which Madam de Maintenon, the widow of Scarron, "the cripple by misfortune and the scoffer by choice," counselled a scapegrace nephew to purchase, and with the letter of advice sent one hundred thousand livres, adding the mocking truth, that the flight of the Huguenots would enable him to get their lands for a trifle. Be this as it may, M. de Montaigne was a gentleman whose Norman ancestry had already been crossed with Saxon blood, for he was the great grandson of the celebrated French essayist, Michel de Montaigne, one of whose parents is said to have been of English descent. Moreover it may be presumed, that he was a gentleman of exact means and of assured condition, who probably had a taste for rural life and some acquaintance with agricultural pursuits, for he avoided the cities and towns, where his countrymen for the most part settled, and purchased a small estate in a quiet part of the county of Norfolk, known as Thwaite Hall, and situated, if we mistake not, about ten miles from the city of Norwich. His society, we may easily suppose, was attractive to the resident gentry, whose tastes most probably inclined them to sympathize with what was bold in thought and heroic in conduct. Moreover, their new protestant acquaintance may have possessed, in addition to his religious principles, social qualifications of a popular kind, for he had seen enough to be amusing, and suffered enough to be admired.

The rustic dialect spoken by the natives of what was anciently an important part of the kingdom of the East Angles, though by no means deficient in music, is, even at this day, of a peculiar and distinctive kind. But at the time M. de Montaigne settled in their midst, those peculiarities were much more marked than they are now, and therefore his neighbours were probably a good deal embarrassed by their efforts to articulate his name, as the pure Norfolk tongue needs a little judicious educating before it cleverly masters the French accent. The Huguenot immigrant no doubt possessed the grace of courtesy, which his descendants have inherited, and it is therefore probable that, like many of his countrymen who settled in the British Islands, he resolved, from considerations of convenience, or perhaps from choice, to become a citizen of the country that had given him shelter; to be in name, as well as in fact, an Englishman; and it may have been for this reason, as well as from feelings of regard for his new friends, that he substituted the exact English equivalent for his French name, for waving any desire to be Mr. Hill, or Mr. Upland, he, and his descendants, thenceforward became known in England and many of her dependencies by the surname which they bear. The name, it is true, has provoked many pleasantries and occasioned some puns, nevertheless it has been borne with high honour and marked distinction by men whose memories will not die—by bishops, priests and soldiers of the race.

The family seems to have clung very steadily to the country in which they first settled, for though in the middle of the last century Thwaite Hall passed into other hands, the descendants of those who once owned it continued to reside in Norfolk. A son of the first immigrant, as we conjecture, succeeded to the county property; at all events he married in England, and died in early life, leaving a widow and two sons, the youngest of whom, the Rev. Jacob Mountain, studied for the Church, and graduated at Caius College, Cambridge. Having completed his University course, and been admitted to holy orders, he made a pleasant visit to the county of Essex, and in the year 1781 married Elizabeth Mildred Wale Kentish, co-heiress with two sisters of Little Bardfield Hall in that county. The Hall is, or was, situated in the "Hundred of Dunmow," celebrated alike in painting and story for what has been termed "The Custom of Dunmow," a custom instituted, it is said, in the days of the Plantagenet Kings, by one of the descendents of Walter Fitz-Walter. The custom is a semi-religious one, and it was formerly accompanied with certain conventual rites. It consisted in the delivery of a flitch, or gammon, of bacon to any married couple in the "Hundred of Dunmow," who, having been united for a year and a day, would, on their knees, take the following quaint rhythmical oath:

"You shall swear, by custom of confession,
 That you never made nuptial of transgression,
 Nor since you were married man and wife,
 By household brawls or contentious strife,
 Or otherwise, at bed or at board,
 Offended each other in deed or in word;
 Or since the Parish Clerk said Amen,
 Wished yourselves unmarried again;
 Or in a twelvemonth and a day,
 Repented not in thought any way,
 But continued true in thought and desire,
 As when you joined hands in holy quire;
 If to these conditions, without any fear,
 Of your own accord you will freely swear,
 A whole gammon of bacon you shall receive,
 And bear it hence, with love and good leave,
 For this is the custom at Dunmow, well known,
 Though the pleasure be ours, the bacon's your own."

The last recorded celebration of the "Custom of Dunmow," so far as we can discover, took place in 1751, for we decline to take account of some modern and we may add indecent satires on the ancient "custom," when the flitch of bacon was awarded to a worthy man who bore what in most other English counties would be thought the singular, but scarcely euphonious name of John Shakeshanks, but in the county of Essex, where odd names abound, it would probably occasion no comment. Thirty-one years later, judging from the touching and beautiful record of a loving life which the Rev. Armine Mountain has published, the prize might most fittingly have been claimed by the Rev. Jacob Mountain and his wife, the co-heiress of little Bardfield Hall, had they thought fit to offer themselves as candidates for such rustic honours.

On his marriage, the Rev. Jacob Mountain was preferred to the living of St. Andrew's, Norwich. Subsequently he was chosen by Dr. Tomline, then Bishop of Lincoln, as his Lordship's examining chaplain, and so highly was he esteemed by that gifted prelate, that he was presented by him to the living of Buckden, in Huntingdonshire, hard by his own palace; for at that day, and until a recent period, the official residence of the Bishop of Lincoln was at Buckden. We may note in passing that his friendship and connection with the Bishop of Lincoln were, in all probability, the direct cause of Dr. Mountain's preferment to the See of Quebec, for Dr. Tomline had not only been the tutor, but also the private secretary of the younger Pitt, and hence it may be presumed that the latter consulted the former when the novel duty was imposed on him of making choice of a fitting person to fill the important office of Bishop of the Anglican Church in Canada. Six children—four sons and two daughters—were the issue of the marriage of the Rev. Jacob Mountain with his wife. Three sons took holy orders, and the fourth adopted the profession of arms. The last mentioned was the late Colonel Armine Mountain, C.B., Adjutant General in India, and Aid-de-Camp to the Queen.

George Jehoshaphat Mountain, the second son and the subject of this sketch, was born at Norwich on the 27th of July, 1789. The period was noteworthy, for a new emigration led by the last Prince of Condé of the direct line, had just commenced from France. One century earlier thousands fled from that fair land, pursued by the intolerance of religious persecution. Then, thousands in like manner, fled, pursued by the savagery of political licentiousness. The fugitives in both cases may be said to have suffered for conscience sake, but in the latter there were not wanting the evidences of what seemed to be a terrible retribution, for the Church party which, in the seventeenth century, had persecuted without pity, in the eighteenth century was outlawed without mercy.

Norwich is rich in sacred memories, and the historic atmosphere which pervaded it seemed to exert no inconsiderable influence on the career of the newly-born child. It was the birth-place of Archbishop Parker, who, in 1533, the year after the first Prince of Condé, the chief of the Huguenots, was born, was charged with the care of the Princess Elizabeth, the future Queen of England. The Archbishop's services in promoting the Reformation, we need scarcely remark, are most reverently cherished in the Anglican Church. The saintly Joseph Hall, the author of "The Contemplations on the Old and New Testament Scriptures," was the Bishop of Norwich at the period of the Great Rebellion; and, the year after George Jehoshaphat Mountain was born, the learned Dr. George Horne, who wrote the Commentaries on the Psalms, was translated to that See. How deeply the principles of Archbishop Parker, and the sentiments and opinions of Bishops Hall and Horne, were to influence the mind and character of George Jehoshaphat Mountain, may, with little difficulty, be conjectured by those who in after years possessed his friendship; who had the opportunity of observing his character, of listening to his teachings, and of studying his works.

Contemporary biography is necessarily written under great disadvantages, for while a man lives his history is incomplete, and consequently all criticism with respect to it must be imperfect, and may be unfair. The like objection cannot be urged for the same reason with respect to those who have passed away; nevertheless, with regard to such persons when only recently deceased, a difficulty of a somewhat analogous kind may be found to exist. It is probable that the worth and service of one who falls as it were in harness, are never less accurately known than at or within a comparatively short time after his death. The grave, it is true, separates such an one from the past, but the newly-made mound, in its unsettled freshness seems to testify that the tenant who slumbers there has not as yet become the property of the future. Contemporaries who have lived with him or jostled against him on the same highway, will regard his character from a point less elevated than that from which posterity will observe it. Distance may be said to exert a contrary influence on moral and on natural landscapes. In the former case, the wider field of observation brings out incidents and features that were in some degree crowded or confused when closely inspected. Indeed, the end of a life may represent but the beginning of a work. We know, for example, little of the underground contributions to a rill before it is filtered through the rock, neither may we at first suspect, what perchance will be found to be true, that the crystal current which brightens the wayside, giving beauty to nature and comfort to man, is neither more nor less than the far-away source of some important river. Hence it is difficult, apart from the aid which time and observation afford, to extract from what seem to be the ordinary objects of every day life, the germ and origin of great results. Such thoughts, or thoughts akin to them, occurred to us as we read the touching memoir of the late Bishop of Quebec, to which we have already referred; for, notwithstanding our veneration for a character that seemed so stainless and was so pure, the impression forced itself on our minds that posterity would appreciate more accurately than his contemporaries have done, the patient and heroic virtues of his saintly life. The work, though attuned to the monotone key to which sacred biography is too commonly pitched and too frequently spoiled, is nevertheless as it seems to us, pleasantly put together, in the somewhat desultory way in which we string beads, for it is more conspicuous for the beauty of its parts than for the perfection of its plan. The chronological chain has been tamely constructed of sombre colours, while the numerous settings are severely free from the suspicion of decoration. It may have been that like a skilled lapidary of earlier days, Mr. Armine Mountain has been careful not to withdraw attention from the gems to the jeweller. He seems and perhaps justly, to have felt that such moral brilliants as those which he was required to set, needed little aid from his art, no glow from his fancy and no gloss from his genius. A reverential calm pervades the work, and perhaps necessarily so, for criticism, by a son of his father, would be out of place, and could by no means have been looked for with respect to one so honored and so beloved. It is probable that the tie of kindred, as well as the close personal and professional intercourse between the father and son, may have placed restraint on the latter, lest, peradventure, from the intensity of his affection, he should speak with unguarded rapture of one who averted his face when men praised him, and was always best satisfied with the language of humility. Nevertheless, the public is deeply indebted to Mr. Mountain for the narrative he has furnished, and for the insight it affords of his father's character and life. Such a narrative is encouraging as well as instructive, for it shows how nearly, even in this world, a good man may approach the kingdom of God. It illustrates the way in which heavenly excellence may control human exertion, and by what discipline the heart of the creature may be fitted and prepared for the abode of the Creator. But when we look from the subject of the memoir to the great purpose for which that subject lived and worked; when we think of the fruits which such labours may be expected to yield; when we look beyond the present to the generations to come, then the opinion we have expressed comes home to us with irresistible force. Posterity will appreciate the Bishop's work more truly, and offer to his memory the incense of a deeper veneration than any which has been paid by those who knew him best. Our admiration for the labours of the saintly missionary will be as nothing compared with their gratitude who, in times future, shall enter upon the fruit of those labours. We eulogize the herald who went, while they will extol the messenger who came with "glad tidings of great joy." Then, perchance, new biographers will arise, who unembarrassed by the restraints of affection, or the consideration of filial reserve, shall narrate, in the passionate language of devout gratitude, what the subject of this memoir did and endured for the generation of their fathers; what he did, before science had made crooked places straight and rough places smooth—before commerce had civilized, or man had settled in the remote portions of his See; what he did for the Indians of Red River, for the fishermen of Labrador, and for the friendless immigrants which Europe annually cast on the shores of America. The lives of the Missionary Bishops of the Anglican Church is a work yet to be written. At present, such narratives must be sought for in detached forms only; but when such a book is written, and the maps traced with the travels and journeyings of each prelate, then will men marvel at what, in their ignorance, some have been found to make light of;—the privations and perils, the self-denial and sacrifice, the labour and sufferings of those who, in obedience to the requirements of their office and ministry, have striven to carry the Gospel to every creature. In what follows we shall have occasion to make frequent reference to, and to borrow largely from, Mr. Mountain's memoir,* and we can only hope that our appropriation of his

---

* A Memoir of George Jehoshaphat Mountain, D.D., D.C.L., late Bishop of Quebec, compiled (at the desire of the Synod of that Diocese) by his son, Armine W. Mountain, M.A., Incumbent of St. Michael's Chapel, Quebec.

researches will quicken the desire of many to become better acquainted with those researches.

The Georgian era of our national history as it has been termed, was a season of severe humiliation to the English Church. Few Christian people refer to that period without shame on one hand and surprise on the other, that a Church so tried and slighted, so abused and maltreated, so hindered in her influence and so dwarfed in her growth, as the Church of England was by the earlier sovereigns of the House of Hanover, should not have been wholly, instead of partially cast down. The story of our conquest and colonization of North America and " the Indies," very fairly represents the religious indifference of that scandalous period. Little was thought, and less was done, for the moral and spiritual welfare of the colonists. The clergymen were few in number, and, at the time of the rebellion of the thirteen American Provinces there was no Bihops of the Anglican Church on the American continent. In 1784, the Clergy of Connecticut elected the Rev. Samuel Seabury to be their Bishop, but that estimable man, having sought and failed to obtain consecration at Lambeth, turned from the affluent Church of England, to the " Suffering and Episcopal Church of Scotland," from whose poor and despised Bishops he received his mitre. Thus it happened that the first Bishop of the Episcopal Church in the United States received consecration at the hands of the Bishops of the Episcopal Church of Scotland. Previous to the independence of the United States, all Church organization in that country was out of the question, and Episcopal ordinances as a matter of course, were never administered. In 1789, the Bishopric of

Nova Scotia was created, and on the 7th July, 1793, the Right Rev. Jacob Mountain was consecrated as the first Bishop of Quebec. Shortly afterwards, accompanied by his wife and their four children, her two sisters, his elder brother, his wife, and their children, the new prelate embarked, and after a voyage of thirteen weeks, as the biographer quaintly observes, "the thirteen Mountains arrived at Quebec on All Saints' day." The cargo, to continue the phraseological pleasantry, was exceptional; but as England and France were then at war, it is probable the unusual delay was due to the fact that the ship was a convoy, or that she sailed under convoy, and not to the load of Mountains with which she was freighted. The fleet of merchant ships which accompanied the Bishop to the seat of his Bishopric, in all probability carried many a French royalist, both priest and layman, to the shelter of British soil. It was a curious reversal of the exodus of the previous century, and well calculated to provoke the thought it received and the charity it produced. Then, France cast out her workers and made Protestant Europe rich by means of their labour, now France expelled her idlers and made her best blood eat the bitter bread of dependence, that was nevertheless very heartily bestowed by the hereditary enemies of their race. No wonder that the Anglican Bishop, on his arrival, was met by the Gallican Bishop, who made him welcome with a kiss on both cheeks. Enmity had been disarmed by kindness, and hence the ecclesiastical representatives of the two peoples received one another with the courtesy which, under the circumstances, might have been expected from gentlemen, and prelates, of the churches of England and France.

CHAPTER SECOND.

> At church, with meek and unaffected grace,
> His looks adorn'd the venerable place:
> Truth from his lips prevail'd with double sway,
> And fools who came to scoff, remain'd to pray—
> The service past, around the pious man,
> With steady zeal, each honest rustic ran;
> E'en children follow'd, with endearing wile,
> And pluck'd his gown to share the good man's smile.
> His ready smile a parent's warmth express'd,
> Their welfare pleased him, and their cares distress'd;
> To them his heart, his love, his griefs, were given,
> But all his serious thoughts had rest in heaven.
>
> *The Deserted Village.*—GOLDSMITH.

ON his arrival the Anglican Bishop proceeded to Woodfield, a very picturesque residence that had been secured for him in the neighbourhood of Quebec. Here the boyhood of his sons was passed; here too they acquired their love for the beauties of nature, which was so peculiarly apparent in the tastes and inclinations of the subject of this memoir. The Rev. Armine Mountain mentions that the first Bishop of Quebec makes frequent allusion in his journal " of walks with the children before breakfast," and although such entries for the most part are of a general rather than of a special character, yet there are occasional notices of incidents in the quiet life of Woodfield which are not without interest. Such a one may be picked out of the notes of the 28th March, 1796. "On this day George began his Latin Grammar." The study which the Bishop commenced on that day was a source of unalloyed happiness to him to the end of his life. The Greek and Latin poets, we have been informed, were almost within his convenient reach, and a day rarely passed without some readings in the cherished books of his college days. Indeed, we are elsewhere told that the few books the Bishop was able to take with him on his visitation tours, always included two or three Greek and Latin authors. His two coat pockets were the abiding places of at least two books, for the curious might have found a Bible in one and a small edition of Cicero in the other. Sometimes in the hold of a fishing smack, sometimes in a bark canoe, and frequently in the hut of a backwoodsman, the Bishop would find instruction as well as happiness in reading what had been said at Rome before the Great Teacher performed His miracles in Palestine or preached His sermon on the mount.

At the age of sixteen, George was sent with his elder brother, both of whom had previously been confirmed by their father, to Little Easton in the county of Essex, England, where under the tuition of the clergyman of the parish they pursued their studies until they entered Trinity College, Cambridge, where the younger brother took his degree in 1810. He then became a candidate for, but failed to obtain a Fellowship, in Downing College, Cambridge, but he acquitted himself so well that the then Professor of Greek, Dr. Monk, one of his Examiners, afterwards Bishop of Gloucester, expressed a wish to recommend him for the office of

Principal of a College in Nova Scotia, for which office that prelate, speaking from what he had observed of his scholarship, thought Mr. Mountain especially fitted.

In the following year, he returned to Quebec, where he became his father's secretary and studied for the holy ministry under his guidance. On the 2nd of August, 1812, he was admitted to deacon's orders, and appointed to assist his cousin, the Rev. Salter Mountain, at that time the clergyman of the parish and chaplain of the Bishop. In the following year, 1813, he attended the Bishop on his triennial visitation of the diocese. His uncle, the Bishop's elder brother, was the resident clergyman at Montreal. At the period of this visitation, there were only seven clergymen in Lower Canada, four of whom bore the name, and belonged to the family of Mountain.

On the sixteenth of January, 1814, the deacon of the previous year was admitted to priest's orders, and on the eighteenth of the same month he was licensed as evening lecturer at the cathedral. On the second of August following, being the anniversary of his ordination, the *Quebec Gazette*, as we have little doubt, announced that the Rev. G. J. Mountain was married, by the Bishop, to Mary Hume, the third daughter of Deputy Commissary General Thompson. Immediately after his marriage he went to Fredericton, where he had been appointed rector by the Bishop of Nova Scotia. On his arrival in that town, he received the further appointments of chaplain of the troops and chaplain of the Legislative Council.

We do not know in what way the newly-married pair were received at the rectory, or how the rector was inducted, but the manner of their approach to the town was the reverse of ostentatious, and bore no marks of either " carnal vanity " or worldly display. Having, for example, arrived at St. John by a somewhat eccentric, geographical course, the travellers supposed that the rest of their way would have been tolerably smooth and free from impediments. But the chapter of adventure was destined to finish consistently. There were no steamboats in those days, and therefore advantage had to be taken of any craft the travellers could find to convey them to Fredericton. But the little vessel in which they ascended the river was unequal to the journey, as it went ashore ten miles below the wished-for haven. There was nothing for it but to push on as best they could. Having, therefore, after the manner of itinerent hay-makers, put up a small bundle of clothing for immediate service, the new rector and his young wife landed on the contiguous shore, and looked about them, if not for succour, at least for transport. A small floating contrivance, which answered the purpose of a ferry, was at length discovered, and, being " manned " by two black women of marine tastes and muscular qualifications, the travellers were at length landed at the desired haven. Under such exceptional circumstances did the Rector of Fredericton take possession of his rectory.

After residing at Fredericton for nearly three years the Rector resigned the living and returned to Quebec. On his arrival he was appointed " Bishop's Official " and also what was then called " Officiating clergyman of Quebec," for it was not until 1821 that the Protestant parish of

Quebec was erected by letters patent, and consequently it was not until then that he properly became the rector. In the last mentioned year he was also appointed Archdeacon of Lower Canada. From that time, we may, in a more especial manner, date the career of charity and piety which was evermore to be associated with his memory, and which was to end only with his life. He commenced wisely, for his earliest act was to establish intimate relations with the Venerable Societies for Promoting Christian Knowledge, and for Propagating the Gospel. To this end, he lost no time in appointing a diocesan committee in connection with the committee of the first mentioned society. His second act was to establish at Quebec, national schools for girls and boys. Early in January, 1818, he commenced as a simple missionary, and afterwards continued as Archdeacon, to visit the out-lying portions of the diocese. Such work he found to the end of his career to be full of attraction and encouragement, for in heart and soul he was the *beau idéal* of a missionary.

In 1819, on his father's recommendation he received the degree of D.D. from the Archbishop of Canterbury, and in the same year he was appointed, by the government, a member of "The Board for the advancement of learning in Canada," in which capacity he visited and inspected schools. In July, 1820, he accompanied his father in what was his first, and the Bishop's last, visitation of the Upper Canada portion of the diocese. The physical, moral, and social changes wrought in fifty years are sufficiently striking, but the primitive state of the Province at the period referred to may be gathered from a trifling incident that was noted by Mr. Mountain at Cornwall. Finding it troublesome to call for his servants, the Bishop said to the maid at the inn, "Pray is there any bell here?" "Yes, Sir." "Where is it?" "Sir," said the maid, with unaffected simplicity, "it is in the Church." A house bell apparently belonged to a state of civilization that Cornwall had not then reached.

It was in the course of his earliest Archdeaconal visitation that Dr. Mountain met with the Honorable and Rev. Dr. Stewart, a man of noble birth, gentle manners and simple piety, who is elsewhere spoken of by the former as "the boast and blessing" of the Canadian Church. Without ostentation or display, in the quietest manner and for the purest ends, that estimable clergyman had left scenes and associations which are commonly regarded as among the prime charms of life, for the purpose of converting the Indians of Canada from the errors of a pagan creed, and of instructing the more savage whites of the wild woods, the trappers and hunters of the new world, in the principles of the Christian faith. Between men of such gentle tastes, such humble minds, and such ripe religious principles, a friendship arose which was as beautiful as it was pure. Like all good works, that friendship was continued as it was begun, in singleness of purpose and sincerity of heart; and in after years, when it passed from a fact to a recollection, the touch of death did not quench its glow or the silence of the grave extinguish its glory; for, to the latest moment of his life, Bishop Mountain was accustomed to speak of Bishop Stewart in tones of holy rapture, not only as a Saul among the prophets, but also as a chief among friends. It is beautiful to note how thoroughly the alloy of mere worldly ambition was exorcised and expelled from the hearts and minds of those saintly men ; each seemed to desire the other's elevation and his own abasement, for both were content to serve as neither of them wished to rule. If any rivalry existed it was the rivalry of humiliation, for each seemed to be only anxious that the other should be preferred to the Bishopric. Thus, when the plan of separating the Diocese fell through, and when Dr. Stewart succeeded to the undivided See, he was unremitting in his efforts to obtain as his suffragan his loved and cherished friend, the subject of this memoir.

The Clergy Reserve question was, as a matter of course, a question of great importance, though, in territorial extent, not of equal value to the Anglican Church in Lower Canada as it was in Upper Canada. But the principle involved was the same in both Provinces, and the agitation and settlement of it included, as early as the year 1822, the duty of sending to England a representative of the rights of the Church, and of the claims of her ministers. The Archdeacon, Dr. Mountain, had been designated to that duty, but for sufficient reason he obtained leave to excuse himself, and at the same time to impose the responsibility on Dr. Stewart. In truth such services, though undertaken as matters of duty, were in the highest degree distasteful to him, for he was constitutionally disinclined to contend or to strive for mere temporalities. Nevertheless, such disinclination was not allowed to master him, for he wrote " I am unalterably convinced, however, of the duty lying upon us to keep watch and ward in defence of our Zion, and to sally out, if the proceedings of the other party render it necessary. But it would seem to human weakness a happier lot for a clergyman to have, as Chillingworth says, 'no enemies but the devil and sin.' Mine seems so different a case that I shall be fit for 'treason, stratagems, and spoils,' if I continue to be exercised in the sort of struggle to which our Church is exposed." The exercise, unfortunately for his peace, was continued for years, but the qualifications playfully referred to, were never attained. There was no guile in his nature and strife was foreign to his taste. He was not an adept in the use of mere secular weapons. The serpent could not lodge in a nature where the dove only had made her nest. This may have been, perhaps it was, a misfortune as well as a weakness, but nevertheless it was a grace the more beautiful for its rarity, and a virtue the more excellent for the difficulty of its attainment. With respect to the late Bishop, his biographer says the necessary forms of business were distasteful to him; he shrank from "diplomacy" and shunned "Parliamentary" or other work, that required address for its success. In fact, to preach the Gospel was his delight as well as his duty, and to be instrumental "in turning many to righteousness" was the aim as well as the solace of his life.

In 1821, on the arrival of the charter of McGill College, Montreal, the Bishop, believing it to be his duty so to do, submitted a plan for its establishment as a university. This plan received the approval of two Governors-in-Chief, the Duke of Richmond and the Earl of Dalhousie. The recommendation of the Archdeacon, the subject of this sketch, for Principal, was not only cordially approved of by those noblemen, but it was heartily commended by the Lieut. Governor of Upper Canada, Sir Peregrine Maitland, as well as by other persons of mark in both Provinces. Two years afterward, the Archdeacon was nominated Honorary Professor of Divinity and Principal of the College, which office he held until 1835. We have neither space nor inclination to speak of the controversies which subsequently arose, or dwell on the history of the College from the point of departure at which it was started, to the point of divergence which it ultimately reached. No doubt, grave mistakes were made in later years, with respect to the patronage of the College, and a weapon was thus offered to the spoiler by those who considered themselves the guardians of the spoil. But without reviving any uncomfortable discussion, let us charitably hope that the will of the founder of that noble institution has been faithfully interpreted by the will of the people, and that his benevolent intentions, if not positively, have at least negatively been respected in the statutes of the University which bears his name and was created by his benevolence.

In the year 1825, by desire of his father, and at the request of the Clergy Reserve corporations of Upper and Lower Canada, the Archdeacon again went to England. His chief object was to represent the claim of the Anglican Church in the matter of the Clergy Reserves, but incidentally he was to express his father's pious wish to be relieved of a portion of the cares of his bishopric. To this end he was instructed to suggest that the extensive diocese of Quebec, which then represented almost half a continent, should be separated in two parts, and each part erected into a separate bishopric. The alternative, in case such a plan should be considered objectional, was to recommend the Rev. Dr. Stewart to be associated with his father in the administration of the See. In either case, Bishop Mountain offered to relinquish £1,000 per annum of his official income, as his contribution towards the much desired object. Whether such a plan would have been carried out or not, does not clearly appear, as during the currency of the negotiation, the high minded prelate, at whose instance it was mooted, found relief in the rest that comes to all. He departed this life on the eighteenth June, 1825, unattended, as the narrator adds, with filial pathos, by any of his sons. The Archdeacon turned mournfully from his unfulfilled mission, sorrow-stricken and disappointed. In the solitude of his state room, and with his face towards home, he indulged, as was his custom when his heart was full, a poet's privilege, and breathed his thoughts in verse. One stanza of the fifteen which have been preserved, will show his tender anxiety, and explain the reason for his importunate appeal to his ship to "speed! speed!" for

> A widow gray;
> His mother dear, will want her son;
> Alas! that in that mournful day;
> Of all her four, she clasp'd not one.

The death of Bishop Mountain relieved the English Ministry of the responsibility of doing something, and afforded them the delicious leisure, which they thoroughly enjoy, of letting things alone. The physical pleas of age and infirmity might have provoked kindness as well as sympathy when the higher moral considerations, it is to be feared, would have had no influence in moving them to action. In the former case, from sheer humanity they might have endeavoured, and possibly with little delay, to do their duty towards man, while in the latter, from motives of convenience, they would have postponed any effort to do their duty towards God. Death cut the knot which diplomacy had left untied, and reversed, so to speak, the obligations of the hour. Instead of troubling themselves to consider how assistance should be given to an aged Bishop, they only felt themselves called on to find a more youthful successor, whose physical strength would place him beyond the requirements of physical assistance. In choosing Dr. Stewart as such successor, the authorities probably considered that they had found one in all respects suited to the office.

Ten years passed away when, in 1835, the Archdeacon was again sent to England, the objects being the same as those which made his former visit necessary; namely, the settlement of the Clergy Reserve question, and the necessity for procuring further Episcopal assistance in the diocese. Bishop Stewart had broken down and in turn needed help. He was most anxious that the Archdeacon, whom he dearly loved and affectionately called his "right hand," should be appointed suffragan. The latter was more than disinclined to accept the duty, for his desire from first to last was to serve and not to rule. He only yielded when Bishop Stewart emphatically declared he would have no one else. His consecration as coadjutor took place on the fourteenth January, 1836, under the title of Bishop of Montreal. On the twelfth of September, 1836, he arrived as suffragan to Bishop Stewart. Ten days afterwards, the last mentioned Prelate was compelled by illness to go to England; and he never returned, for becoming gradually weaker he entered into rest in the month of July, of the following year, 1837. Thus, in spite of every effort to the contrary, the subject of this sketch became the third Bishop in succession of the undivided Diocese of Canada.

Chapter Third.

I know Thee, bright and morning star,
    I own Thee for my only guide;
But ah! I view Thee from afar,
    Between are waters rough and wide.

A rest remains, a heavenly rest:
    No death, no pain, no sorrowing sigh;
Chased every care from every breast,
    Wiped every tear from every eye.

The day is near, far spent the night:
    Christ will his followers' place prepare;
The Lord our everlasting light;
    Our God shall be our glory there.

Thoughts in verse by the Right Rev.
G. J. Mountain, Bishop of Quebec.

ON two occasions had the Bishop of Quebec crossed and recrossed the Atlantic, for the purpose of moving the authorities in England to create a new diocese, and appoint a second Bishop for the Anglican Church in Canada, but hope was wearily deferred, as success seemed rather to elude than to reward exertion, for notwithstanding the praiseworthy importunities repeated during a period of nearly twenty years, Dr. Mountain found himself the sole successor to the ecclesiastical heritage of his dear friend, Bishop Stewart. The immense Diocese of Quebec still represented the Provinces of Upper and Lower Canada; it still included the territories from the Gulf of St. Lawrence to Lake Superior, and for spiritual purposes, if the phrase be not a satire, the unexplored, though by no means uninhabited, wastes between Lake Superior and the Pacific Ocean. Nevertheless, Dr. Mountain accepted the trust. It is probable that he accounted himself honoured, if not happy, in succeeding to the duties as well as to the aspirations of his predecessors in the Bishopric. Those duties were familiar duties, for they included the work of reconciling man to God, and those aspirations were glorious aspirations, for they included the obligation of planting the reformed faith in its integrity throughout the British Possessions in America. Such duties and such aims had fastened themselves on Dr. Mountain's affections with undying tenacity, and consequently they took their place among the controlling desires of his holy life. The especial object for which the Bishop had been required to make two voyages to England, very naturally became a subject of serious study. Incidentally, and in connection with that study, his thoughts would necessarily be directed to the Church as a divine organization for the spiritual blessing of individuals, and for the moral welfare of society. Highly interesting notes on these subjects were found by his biographer among the Bishop's papers, which went far to show that long before "the Oxford movement" was commenced many of the important questions that were slowly ripening in the minds of Oxford men had engaged the serious thoughts of one who was far removed from the quickening sympathies of University life;—of one who, amidst difficulties and discouragements was doing the work of an Evangelist in the wilds of Canada. As the missionary archdeacon journeyed over the moral waste which the protestant settlements in Canada represented, his devout mind must have been sensibly affected as he noted the unfulfilled duties of the Church of which he was a minister. Where, he might have asked in the passionate language of expostulation, "where is the seal of her commission and where are the signs of her Apostleship, where are the men, who by their office and ministry we account the accredited successors of those chosen ones, on whose heads were laid the divine hands, whose brows were bedewed with the divine breath and whose souls were solaced with the assurance of the divine presence;—where are they?" The Church of England at that day, and until recent times, appeared content to be English and isolated, respectable and exclusive, and to be little or nothing more. The Scriptural duty of "lengthening her cords and strengthening her stakes!" was scarcely more than a rhetorical figure. The parliamentary privileges of her spiritual rulers awakened more concern than the higher duty of sending such rulers, staff in hand, to the uttermost parts of the earth. The satire of Macaulay was the more incisive for its proximity to truth; for the Church "by law established," was as much an insular institution as the "Court of Common Pleas." The English race reproduced itself abroad as well as at home, in the colonies as well as in the Mother Country; but the English Church apparently had no such re-productive power. The Bishop of Oxford, on a public occasion, is reported to have said: "The Presbytery and the Diaconate were evolved out of the Episcopate, and not the Presbytery and the Diaconate run up into the Episcopate," and it was, probably among other and more grievous causes, the indifference to this truth, and the consequent disregard of the primitive plan, that occasioned the declension in the number of church members in England, and their too general alienation from the church when they settled in the colonies.

Bearing in mind what Bishop Mountain had said and done on the subject of extending and increasing the Colonial Episcopate, by labouring for the integrity, if not for the independence, of the Colonial Church, it will scarcely be presumptuous for us to conjecture that on no public occasion, in the course of his long and useful life, was he more thoroughly thankful than on the 21st of April, 1853, when, on the invitation of the Archbishop of Canterbury, he attended a meeting held at Willis' Rooms, "for the furthur extension of the Episcopate in the Colonies and Dependancies of the British Crown." For nearly twenty years, as we have said elsewhere, Dr. Mountain had laboured singly and almost alone, but without success, to add one Bishop to the immense Diocese of Canada, and yet before he entered into rest, he was permitted the joy of seeing what, including Red River and British Columbia, was once his own Diocese, sub-divided into six distinct Bishoprics, to which a seventh has since been added, and this seventh diocese, we may observe in passing, is now served by a greater number of clergymen than were in orders in the whole of Canada, when Dr. Mountain succeeded to the Bishopric in 1836.

An increase to the Colonial Episcopate was not the only question that had engaged the Bishop's thoughts, for other subjects almost as important, necessarily flowed from or were included in it. Synodical action, that is, be it remembered, a course of action by which the Bishops of Canada, voluntarily, and without being asked so to do, delegated to the laity, powers which they had theretofore exercised, and which, had they been merely ambitious men, they might still have retained. Such action whether directed by Diocesan or by Provincial Synods was in harmony with Dr. Mountain's opinions and was warmly promoted by his counsel and his influence. Such action represented progress in church organization, for by securing the active co-operation of the laity, it very essentially advanced the cause of union and fellowship by engaging both orders in the business of Church work.

The machinery by which such work was to be carried forward included another advantage which most thoughtful Churchmen desired to attain. The union of Parishes into Dioceses had already been provided for, but the union of Dioceses into provinces, with a Metropolitical See and a Provincial Primate, was a work yet to be accomplished. This final act, to the great satisfaction of the Bishop of Quebec, was graciously allowed by Her Majesty and ratified by Royal letters patent in the year 1860.

"Before honour is humility," contrary to his own wish, at the imperative desire of his dear friend, Bishop Stewart, Dr. Mountain accepted the responsibility of the Episcopate and the spiritual oversight of a Diocese. When Canada was erected into an Ecclesiastical Province, the Bishop of Quebec was most properly, as a matter of right, the prelate whose advice was sought for to direct the new movement. The office of Metropolitan was not, we are informed, offered to him, but we learn from Mr. Mountain's narrative that the contemplated arrangements would have necessitated his acceptance of it, had he not interposed and created a change in those arrangements. Furthermore, we learn that he anticipated the course of events by writing privately to the Archbishop of Canterbury to recommend that the appointment should be conferred on the Bishop of Montreal. Thus as his biographer says : "the appointment of the Metropolitan was in entire accordance with the wishes of the Bishop of Quebec." We gather further, that the Bishop leaned, and very naturally, to the practice of the Anglican rather than to that of the American Church. He wished for a Metropolitical See as well as a Metropolitan Bishop, for in his address to the Synod of the Diocese he says : "we have full reason I think to be satisfied with the location of the Metropolitan See at Montreal. The situation of that city is central, its wealth and its population greatly surpass those of any other city in British North America, and it is more marked than any other by a general spirit of progress and improvement. Nor is it a circumstance to be counted absolutely for nothing that it now has a really creditable cathedral church, correct in design and beautiful in effect. As far as the person holding office is concerned, all parties must be thoroughly satisfied, but in point of fact it is the place, and not the person nor any personal considerations of whatever kind which ought to determine the choice of the Metropolitan See."

With respect to the proposition which has found favour with some, of transferring the Metropolitical jurisdiction to other Sees, and thus of making the Primate a kind of itenerant, the Bishop of Quebec has left on record a very earnest protest which contains among other arguments, the following reasons against any departure from ancient ecclesiastical usage:

"BECAUSE it is most highly inexpedient and undesirable to introduce into any branch of the Colonial Church any such marked deviation from ancient ecclesiastical and Anglican usage as would be involved in substituting for the office of Metropolitan, properly understood, a sort of ambulatory jurisdiction which would shift about from See to See."

"BECAUSE the city of Montreal is central in point of local situation and is of all cities in the Province, the most populous, the most considerable, the most prosperous and the most increasing."

The dignity which the Bishop of Quebec for very obvious and praiseworthy reasons recommended to be conferred on the City of Montreal, that city does not seem to appreciate, for, if newspaper reports are to be credited, a great number of the churchmen of that city and diocese are striving, and it has been said with a fair promise of success, to get rid of the distinction, because, as it would seem, it rebukes faction and stands in the way of self interest. The meridian of Montreal appears but ill-suited to the reception, much less to the preservation, of Royal favours. That superb city, for example, was selected by Her Majesty as the civil capital of Canada, a selection which politicians disturbed by their passion and lost by their pride. Again it was chosen by the same authority as the ecclesiastical capital of the Anglican Church in British North America, but the members of that Church resident in the city, as well as some who live in the district, seem half inclined to browbeat those who made selection, to degrade their diocese by spurning its honours, and to be angry with the temporal head of the Church for electing it to such distinctions. Such petulance gives rise to more surprize than it ought to do, for a community which, like Esau, made light of its "birthright," is not likely to set much store by "its blessing."

The objection that is commonly, and not unfairly, urged to the mode which has been established by the Synod for filling vacancies as they arise in the Metropolitical See, is, that the Clergy and Laity of the Diocese of Montreal cannot directly and without interference elect the Bishop of their own diocese, and consequently that no one having a cure of souls in the Diocese of Montreal can hope to arrive at the honour of the Episcopate. Although such a view of the case is not severely correct, it nevertheless presents some difficulties that ought not to exist, and that might very conveniently be got rid of, to the great advantage of the Church and without injury to the clergy. But the remedy, we incline to think, should be sought for, elsewhere than in a change of ancient ecclesiastical usage. The Presbyters of the Diocese of Montreal might and certainly ought to enjoy equal facilities with the Presbyters of any other Diocese of winning for themselves "a good degree," but the disability under which they labour should, and we think might be removed without injury to the higher office and without disturbing the natural wish that the presiding officer of the House of Bishops should be taken from the Episcopal order.

It is difficult to believe that the Metropolitans of Canada would attract the respect they should command were they invariably chosen because they were probably the most aged, and possibly the least eligible members of the order. The remedy for many inconveniences and some contradictions, we venture to think, is not to be found either in the abolition of the Metropolitical See or in depriving the House of Bishops of the privilege, which the Lower House of Convocation enjoys, of nominating and electing its own President. On the contrary, redress should be sought for in an entire change of the mode of electing Diocesan Bishops, such a change would not only remove the grievance of which the Clergy of the Diocese of Montreal have some reason to complain, but it would do more, it would secure the Anglican Church in Canada against a recurrence of such scandals as have too generally been associated with the most solemn of her Synodical acts. This is not the place to enlarge upon the question, but we believe it to be within the power of the Canadian Church to amend her canons, in this particular, and by so doing to approach more nearly to the primitive mode of electing Bishops, as nearly as our circumstances will permit, to the forms and ceremonies that were observed by the apostles and as they are narrated in Holy Writ.

The account of the Bishop's services must be sought for, not only in his son's memoirs, not only in the various papers which the subject of that memoir has given to the public, but also in the recollections and traditions which survive and are treasured in the poorer settlements of his diocese. In such places the joy which his visits occasioned was only exceeded by the grief which attended his departure. Struggling immigrants and poor fisher folk who had nothing but love and tears to give, gave both to him as they bade him God speed and saw him beyond their shores. But after all, those interesting papers and those traditions communicate little beyond what he was able to accomplish after his succession to the Bishopric, they tell less, than we long to know, of what he had previously done as Rector and Archdeacon of Quebec. Too little is said of the parish institutions which had been mainly called into existence by his zeal, and placed on a permanent foundation, partly by his contributions, but chiefly by his care—schools for youths, asylums for orphans, homes for the aged, and clothing societies for the poor. It affords scant particulars of his ministerial duties, his four services on Sundays, and his miscellaneous works of charity on week days. Such work as could only have been accomplished by one who had reduced zeal to a system, and had organized his labours, like his alms deeds, on the principle of doing the greatest possible good to the greatest possible number of people.

Again, as we read the account supplied by his biographer of his heroic charity during two memorable seasons of plague and pestilence which, commencing at Quebec, swept over Canada, we seem almost to realize the dramatic portraitures of the sacred scriptures. In thought, we behold the commissioned minister of the Most High standing between the living and the dead, if not to stay the plague, at least to point the plague smitten to Him who had taken the sting from death. The immigrant station at *Grosse-Isle* had been set apart by Government as the receiving station for immigrants who arrived in the pest ships from Europe in the cholera years of 1832-34. The grave-yard of the Island was rapidly filled. The disease seemed to leap across the belt of water that separates that Island from the shore, and having fallen like a fire-brand in Quebec, it spread through the city like a flame. When the cholera broke out in 1832, the population of Quebec amounted to twenty-eight thousand; by the end of July, that is to say, in about two months time, two thousand eight hundred had died. On two consecutive days in June, upwards (thus loosely the record reads) of seventy-five persons were buried by the Rector. Nevertheless, amidst such harassing duty, provision was made for further service. A horse was kept saddled day and night in his stable to enable him or his assistant in the parish to attend to people who resided at a distance from him. Many nights, says his biographer, they were both out, and for whole days unable to return. Again, in 1847, the ship fever, the fatal product of famine in Ireland, was imported into Canada. The Anglican clergy, who were few in number, with devoted zeal took their duty at *Grosse-Isle* week about, the Bishop taking the first week. Most of the clergy sickened, and two of them died of the fever. Their names are worthy of being preserved, and therefore we give them as follow, viz:—

Butler, Rev. J.	Mackie, Rev. G.	Reid, Rev. C. P.
Guerout, Rev. N.	Morice, Rev. C.	Rollet, Rev. C.
Forrest, Rev. C.	Morris, Rev. C. J.	Sutton, Rev. E.
King, Rev. W.	Mountain, Rev. A. W.	Torrance, Rev. J.
Lonsdell, Rev R.	Parkin, Rev. E. C.	Whitten, Rev. A. T.

The trial, we may well imagine, was acute enough, for in the summer of 1847, upwards of five thousand interments took place at the immigrants station at *Grosse-Isle*. "No one liveth to himself or dieth to himself," wrote the heroic Bishop. There was a chivalry as well as a gentleness in his nature which, like expressed virtue, communicated its energy to all. It was the spirit of christian knighthood, of unwavering devotion which animated his heart. Fear was exorcised and cast out by love; and love being the twin of faith, found joy in duty. Exaggerations, either of fact or of metaphor, were equally offensive to the Bishop, but as he has passed away we may say now what could not have been said then, that, like the captives of old, he especially seemed to walk through the fever furnace of that terrible season, and like them, though in another sense, without smell or taint of harm touching him. This spirit of self-sacrifice always shone in his character, and unquestionably added virtue, as well as beauty, to his life. When, for example, the Church Missionary Society was desirous of establishing a Bishopric in the heart of the Red River country, he was the prelate to whom that Society applied to take the exploring journey of nine thousand miles. Doubtless he was happy to go, for the work was mission work, and consequently it was precisely the work in which his soul found comfort. It enabled him to teach and to pray with Indians and half breeds, as well as to lay the foundation of a permanent Bishopric. It was during that journey, in his bark canoe, or beneath the forest shade, he wrote and perchance sang his *Songs of the Wilderness*, a collection of small poems which are bright with beautiful thoughts. Again, some years later, when a difficulty was found to exist with respect to the appointment of a Bishop of Sierra Leone, in consequence of the climate having proved rapidly fatal to more than one occupant of the See, he wrote to the Secretary of the Society for the Propagation of the Gospel to know whether the difficulty had been surmounted; his reason for doing so, as he told his son, was that he intended to offer himself for the post that "he might wipe away the reproach from the Church of England."

The records of such a life increase our admiration of the nature in which that life was clothed. Nevertheless such admiration is qualified with astonishment as we remember how sensibly his charitable works were hindered by some who, nevertheless, had the courage to affect a deeper spirituality of character, and a more intense devotion to the great doctrines of the christian faith than this peerless christian Bishop. Happily we are not required to judge other men, it is enough for us to record that Christ and His church were, it is no exaggeration to say so, the "alpha and the omega," the beginning and the end, the all and in all of the Bishop's life, and hence the discipline of reproach and resistance through which he was required to pass must have been a cruel trial for him to bear. But the beauty of his character on no occasion, as we think, shone more brightly than when it was subjected to these special trials. He was too earnest a man not to respect earnestness. He was too learned a man not to be tolerent to ignorance. He was too wise a man not to make allowance for prejudice. He knew that earnestness, and ignorance, and prejudice, like their opposites, were powers which no ruler could make light of, much less despise. His pious wish was to blend knowledge with virtue, and by overcoming ignorance with wisdom to purify and direct both to the best uses. Two trivial incidents within the writer's recollection will illustrate the Bishop's forbearance and tact as well as his patience and courtesy. The annual report of the Church Society had been written for the secretary of the society who was then too ill to write it himself, and being approved of by the Bishop, it was submitted, as was the custom, to a meeting of the Central Board of that society, that it might be confirmed by that Board before it was presented to the annual meeting. Objections of an irritating and frivolous kind were taken to the report. The Bishop did not rebuke the objectors, but, with great meekness of tone and manner answered their objections. The critics, in point of fact, had no cause for criticism, and they merely shewed temper, and lost tact, in their search for one. A very respectable presbyter, for example, suddenly jumped up, and, apparently labouring under the impression that every product of the pen should either drip with pulpit unction, or be as dry as the dreariest of pulpit oratory, exclaimed (the words are not our words), "Well, my Lord, it would be more satisfactory if the report said less about the church and more about Christ." The observation, of course, provoked a smile which few could suppress, and had the subject been less solemn the smile would have been less subdued. But levity on such an occasion, it may well be supposed, was foreign enough to the reverent mind of the Bishop. With surprizing forbearance, and without any irony of manner or acidity of speech, he explained to the petulant presbyter that the Church Society was an organization wholly and solely established to teach mankind "more about Christ" and His salvation. The objectors had not exhausted their objections. Incidentally the report in question spoke of the sacraments as the "sacraments of grace," whereupon a very earnest, well-meaning layman rose, and with ludicrous indignation exclaimed, "My Lord, I have heard of the sacrament of baptism, and of the sacrament of the Lord's supper, but I never heard of a sacrament of grace!" The Bishop did not say in stern English what his Western brother might have said in broad Scotch, "Sit down, sir, you are talking nonsense," but with great patience and courtesy he dropped his words of kindness, like soothing oil, on the bright bald head of the objector, and explained to him in the words of the catechism, as he might have done to a wayward child, that the sacraments being "outward and visible signs of inward and spiritual grace," were conventionally, and with great propriety, called "sacraments of grace." Again on the "Surplice question," the Bishop had been much pressed by a section of his clergy to make an order to the disadvantage of the black gown. Personally, as we have some reason to think, the Bishop preferred that divine worship should be celebrated in one vestment, and that one the surplice. The absence of disquieting interruptions, the greater simplicity of usage which such arrangements represented, and its closer approach to the canonical direction, harmonized with the lowliness of his character, and perhaps, also, with his recollections of the village custom that, time out of mind, had been observed in many of the country parts of England. But what may have been lawful was not by him deemed to be expedient. The law of the church seemed clear enough but the usage of her ministers had not been uniform. The use of the black gown is probably as much attributable to pride as to principle, for in some parts of England, at least, they were the beneficed clergy, or such only as could afford the luxury, who preached in silk, and not the curates who in the rural districts were frequently too poor to use any other than the linen vestments which the law obliged the churchwardens to provide, but which the law did not compel those officials to keep clean. Hence it commonly happened that the curate's surplice was not only dirty from neglect but it was damp from exposure to the pestilent atmosphere of churches that were neither warmed nor ventilated. However, the gown had acquired a sort of prescriptive right to be considered. The Bishop was a lover of peace as well as a lover of good men and therefore he declined to dignify a ridiculous dispute with an Episcopal direction. It was not for such causes that he would exasperate the weakness of a clergyman or imperil the quiet of the church. A prejudice, unreasonable it may have been, was known to exist in the minds of some of the clergy who were alike respectable and respected for their learning and piety. The Bishop was too wise a man to undervalue prejudice or treat it as of little account, and hence he chose rather to humour, than to excite such weakness, especially as it represented a type of that oldfashioned conservative thought which he at least was not disposed to make light of, much less to ignore. At least one presbyter of the Bishop's diocese, for example, was beset with eccentric opinions on this particular subject which he took no small pains to exhibit. Apparently he liked variety in the matter of dress and thought it charming. On occasion he would appear in five changes of raiment in the course of a morning service. The varieties were accomplished in this way. He did not approve of sitting in the chancel in his surplice, or of sitting in his pew without a gown—but in carrying out his objections he mingled lessons of thrift with lessons of theology, for like Gilpin's wife, he had " a frugal mind," and therefore he wore an old black gown for the depressed service of the pew, and a new black gown for the exalted service of the pulpit. Thus, when the Holy Communion was celebrated, and it happened to be his duty to preach, he twice changed his black gown for the surplice, and twice changed his surplice for some other kind of dress. Though such transformations smack of ritual, they were merely fond conceits, for he who indulged them like most English Churchmen had no relish for ritualistic whimsicalities. Such vagaries are more foolish than hurtful and beneath the serious notice of one who like the Bishop was too much in earnest about things spiritual to waste his advice on the cut of a vestment, the turn of a tippet, or the colour of a robe.

The Bishop's great humility of character, combined with his repeatedly expressed preference for the private station, gave rise to an opinion, more especially among his clergy, which, we think, was more general than accurate, that " he was but an indifferent administrator." The narrative of his life does not sustain this opinion, for, though sorely tried and adroitly assailed, there is no evidence with which we are acquainted of his having spoken unadvisedly or acted indiscreetly. Neither can we discover wherein his adversaries triumphed over him. On the contrary, the seal of success appears to have been most legibly stamped on his labours. The wisdom of his rule was perhaps more real than apparent for it was felt rather than seen. At all events he did not govern too much, or interfere capriciously with either clergy or laity. He was too high bred to use any other language than the language of gentleness, and too well instructed to overlook or to undervalue the apostolic injunction to " be courteous." The Huguenot heritage of religious liberty was not repudiated by the heir of a Huguenot. There was breadth as well as depth in his character. His thoughts harmonized with his actions, and both were generous as well as pure. His heart warmed towards goodness, and it was especially sympathetic towards sincerity. Devout men were gladly welcomed and encouraged to work in his diocese, even though their views on all matters were by no means identical with his. Then, to his honour be it spoken, he appreciated the freedom of the Anglican Church. He was neither a sectarian nor a political Bishop, and hence a man's relation to the church was never represented by him as in any way dependent on his belonging to a particular school of churchmen, or to a particular coterie of politicians. As Dean Goodwin wrote of Bishop Mackenzie, few asked if the Bishop of Quebec were " High church " or " Low church." His work was catholic and meant for mankind and not for a party. It consisted of such work as the Baptist performed when he preached repentance, and of such work as Chillingworth referred to when he said that a clergyman should have no enemies but "the devil and sin." One text, his son informs us, found frequent place in his sermons, and it was almost always printed in capitals: "There is joy in the presence of the angels of God over one sinner that repenteth." His ceaseless aim was to foil the great Tempter of mankind. His means were faith and obedience, and his medicine self-denial and prayer.

But we must pass on, since our space places a restraint on our inclination. During the meeting of the Synod in July, 1862, a resolution of an auticipatory character, was, with great propriety, moved by Mr. W. S. Wurtele, and seconded by the Rev. J. W. Williams, to make arrangements for a Jubilee service on the second of the following month, when the Bishop would complete the fiftieth year of his ministry. We may observe that Mr. Williams was at that time Rector of the juvenile department of the Lennoxville School, a school that was established and conducted under the Bishop's sanction, as a feeder to the university of Bishop's College, Lennoxville. That university was originated by the Bishop, and we can easily believe, what is commonly reported, that it was regarded by him as the greatest of his good works in Canada. The resolution to which we have referred was carried by acclamation, all the members of the Synod rising in their places, and continuing to stand while the subject of it made his acknowledgments. On the second of August following, addresses were presented and a special service of an impressive character was celebrated in the Cathedral, which included the contribution of a purse of money sufficient in amount to found a scholarship in the University of Bishop's College, Lennoxville, to be called the "Mountain Jubilee Scholarship."

Thus, the "ravelled rainbow overhead" with its "crimson pain," and "violet grief," at last dissolved in perfect and untroubled light. Thus was the saintly Bishop enabled to say his *Jubilate Deo*, and join the praises of those elder saints who had not only sung their *Veni Jesu*, but with peaceful resignation had breathed their *Nunc Dimittis*. He might have attuned his faith to song and have exclaimed with fervour :

> "Far out of sight while yet the flesh enfolds us,
> Lies the fair country where our hearts abide ;
> And of its bliss is nought more wondrous told us,
> Than these few words, 'I shall be satisfied.'"

The year of Jubilee was speedily followed by the year of release. "It was, writes his biographer, perhaps, the peacefulness of his diocese and parish, which produced in this year an unwonted, or rather a more uniform cheerfulness of mind, and apparently renewed strength of body." Those who had opposed him had ceased from strife, and consequently he had turned gratefully from the duty of resisting the proud that he might with undisturbed peacefulness minister grace to the lowly. He had, however, recently undergone much hardship and exposure by land and by water, in visiting the outlying and almost inaccessible portions of his diocese, but it seemed that by doing so, a last longing of his soul was satisfied, for he established a mission, and what was better, he sent a missionary to the scattered fishermen on the sterile coast of Labrador. Thus God was bringing him, as his son touchingly observes, "peace at the last." Advent solemnities and Christmas joys were approaching, and both were alike precious to him ; indeed his thoughts never seemed to be more heavenly than when, tinged with the reflections of Advent, they melted into the charities of Christmas. For they were

> Thoughts of His coming—for that joyful day,
> In patient hope I watch, and wait and pray;
> The dawn draws nigh; the midnight shadows flee
> Oh! what a sunrise will that Advent be.

The year in many ways was being crowned with goodness. He had probably mingled his joy with the joys of harvest, while his relish was ripening for the joys of home. The old year of the world was passing away, but a new year of the church had commenced its cycle. The solemn services of Advent, one after another, had been celebrated. Advent, or as it is sometimes called, "The Lesser Lent" had given place to Christmastide, with its "blaze of song," its argosies of happiness, its blessed burden of bright words, its kindly greetings, its family gatherings, its forgetfulness of injuries, its practice of charity, and its old carol of thanksgiving and praise:

> "Glory to God on high—on earth be peace,
> And love towards men of love, Salvation and release."

And the Bishop preached on that grand festival as if he had renewed his youth; or as if his heart had been invigorated and his mind inspired with the very spirit of Christmas. The subject was congenial and suited the season, for it was on the love of God and the joy of Christmas. But, alas! the joy which gladdened the christians of Samaria was to be mingled with bitter memories in the recollections of the christians of Quebec. They were his last words whose face the most of us was never more to see in time. On the following day, the festival of St. Stephen, news went abroad that the Bishop was absent from church. The surprise became anxiety, when it was known that on the two subsequent days, which were also days "to be observed," his place was vacant. Men looked gravely, as if they feared the "sickness was unto death." None ever doubted his love for those among whom his lot had been cast, but few appreciated, until then, how intense was their love for him. In every church of his communion, and in some of the Roman Catholic churches, prayers were offered for his recovery, and no wonder, for the loss with which the community was menaced was only exceeded by the love which it felt. Thirty years of absence had not sufficed to quench the regard which three years of intercourse had created in the hearts of his parishioners at Fredericton, for as a lady resident of that town said to the writer, when speaking of the occasion on which the Bishop revisited them, "the memory of those three years was imperishable."

Prospective, like actual absence, brought with it a sense of loss. Thus it was that the apprehension of his death caused those who knew him best and loved him most, to mourn with a sorrow too sacred to be touched with an intrusive pen. We shall take advantage of the narrative of one who was present, for he has told us in his biography something of that farewell scene. He has told us of the thought and love which divided with hope and death the few last days and hours of the Bishop's life. The goodness of his character was seen not only in his remembrance of great duties, but in his recollection of small kindnesses. He remembered his clergy, and when he could only speak with difficulty, he was able to say, "cheques for the clergy,"—such cheques having reference to the quarterly stipends paid by him to them. Then his wish to see, and to say a few holy words to his servants, who came gratefully and knelt for the blessing they received; and lastly, his love for his children and his children's children. "My children," said the Bishop, "I am dying. I am going to the other world (pointing upwards.) You know how tenderly I have always loved you here," and then he laid his hands on the head of each. The imposition of those dying hands will have left an impression which the wear and tear of time is not likely to efface. About half-past one in the morning of the feast of the Epiphany, 1863, the anniversary of the day on which he commenced his first visitation of his Diocese, he said, 'Lift me up.' "We raised him," continued his biographer, "in our arms, and I felt no more movement than if an infant had fallen asleep on my shoulder, while those who were in front of him saw him gently close his eyes. His family and the diocese were fatherless!"

It is true that all seasons are alike to such as are ready to obey the summons which, sooner or later, death serves upon them; nevertheless, to those whose christian life moves conformably with the chart of the christain year, each season brings a special, as well as a general lesson. The doctrine of the Epiphany, like that of Christmas, is the doctrine of the Incarnation, and it was this doctrine of "God manifest in the flesh," that shone so conspicuously in, and formed such an essential part of, the Bishop's teaching. The Eastern Star which led the wise men to the cradle of the Saviour, was, we may say so without impiety, the pole star of the Bishop's life. The "glittering host" which "bestud the sky" would have lost their brightness to him, if "above and beyond the shining train," his eye of faith could not have rested "on the star of Bethlehem." It was the star which lent poetry to his childhood and peace to his age, which cheered him in his wandering and which lighted him home.

> Ne'er may we lose it from our sight,
> Till all our hopes and thoughts are led
> To where it stays its lucid flight
> O'er our Saviour's lowly bed."

It was his great delight, in spirit and in truth, to draw as nearly as God would permit to " where the young child was;" and whether with the Jewish shepherds or with the Gentile sages, the passionate language of the Prophet, as it is written in the proper lessons for the eve of the Nativity, and for the morning of "the Manifestation," was the lesson of his heart and the prayer of his lips. Like one of the Eastern Magi he seemed to watch for the time when the words of the Evangelical Seer should receive their final accomplishment, when the earth being enclosed with a girdle of truth, nation should answer nation, and with seraphic rapture exclaim, " Arise, shine, thy Light is come, and the Glory of the Lord is risen upon thee."

When the dying Bishop "shut his own eyes" upon earth and earthly things, who shall say that the word *Ephphatha*, once spoken by his compassionate Saviour was not again repeated; who shall say that cloudless light, as well as heavenly rest, are not now his portion in those realms of peace where "the spirits and souls of the righteous await their perfect consummation and bliss?" Of those who loved and respected him and mingled their prayers with the cathedral congregation, or followed his hearse through the January snow, or saw his coffin placed beside the remains of his much beloved wife, in the quiet cemetery at Sillery, some wept silent tears, saying to themselves softly the imperishable words uttered aloud by the unhappy prophet to the princes of Moab—" Let me die the death of the righteous, and let my last end be like his," while others, with the expiring notes of the organ lingering faintly in their ears, and the last holy words of the hymn which had been sung at his funeral lodging sadly in their hearts, repeated to themselves, or to one another, the thrilling syllables of its closing prayer :

<blockquote>Lord, all pitying ; Jesu blest !
Grant *him* THINE eternal rest.</blockquote>

Appendix.

List of persons admitted to Holy Orders by the Right Rev. GEORGE JEHOSHAPHAT MOUNTAIN, D.D., D.C.L., the third Bishop of Quebec.

Names.	Year of Ordination	Names.	Year of Ordination
Allen, Rev. A. A.	1852	* Foster, Rev. J.	1862
Allen, Rev. J. A.	1842	Fothergill, Rev. M. M.	1857
* Antish, Rev. R.	1858	Fulton, Rev. J.	1848
Bancroft, Rev. C.	1843	Gavin, Rev. D.	1848
† Binet, Rev. W.	1854	Gibson, Rev. J.	1839
† Birtch, Rev. R. S.	1853	* Godden, Rev. T.	1862
Bond, Rev. W. B.	1840	* Godfrey, Rev. W.	1839
Bourne, Rev. R. S.	1837	† Greene, Rev. R. J.	1858
Boyle, Rev. F.	1851	Guerout, Rev. N.	1839
Brethour, Rev. W.	1857	Hamilton, Rev. C.	1857
Broome, Rev. F.	1840	Hazard, Rev. H.	1842
Burrage, Rev. H. G.	1848	Helmuth, Rev. I.	1846
† Butler, Rev. J.	1843	* Herchmer, Rev. W. M.	1836
† Carden, Rev. R.	1854	Irwin, Rev. J.	1847
Carey, Rev. J.	1850	Jenkins, Rev. J. H.	1855
Chapman, Rev. T. S.	1848	Johnson, Rev. J.	1858
* Constantine, Rev. J.	1850	* Jones, Rev. C.	1843
* Cookesley, Rev. F. J.	1862	† Jones, Rev. J.	1842
* Cowley, Rev. J.	1841	Jones, Rev. J. W.	1858
† Crosse, Rev. S.	1857	† Jones, Rev. S.	1856
* Crown, Rev. J. M. S.	1848	* Jones, Rev. W.	1844
Cusack, Rev. E.	1837	Judd, Rev. F. E.	1850
Dalziel, Rev. J.	1849	* Kennedy, Rev. T. S.	1858
† Dalziel, Rev. R.	1849	Kemp, Rev. J.	1847
Dawes, Rev. W.	1838	King, Rev. W.	1840
De LaMare, Rev. F.	1850	† Knight, Rev. R.	1836
† De Mouilpied, Rev. J.	1860	Leach, Rev. W. T.	1843
* Devine, Rev. J. A.	1843	* Lewis, Rev. R.	1848
Ellegood, Rev. J.	1848	* Lindsay, Rev. R.	1850
Elliott, Rev. F. G.	1837	Lloyd, Rev. W. V.	1850
Emery, Rev. C. P.	1855	* Lockhart, Rev. A. D.	1850
* Evans, Rev. H.	1843	Lonsdell, Rev. R.	1839
Falloon, Rev. D.	1851	Loucks, Rev. E.	1858
* Fidler, Rev. T.	1839	Lundy, Rev. F. J.	1837
* Flanagan, Rev. J.	1839	† Lyster, Rev. W. G.	1859
* Fletcher, Rev. J.	1846	* Machin, Rev. W.	1849
Forest, Rev. C.	1846	MacMaster, Rev. J.	1858

186   *Appendix.*

List of persons admitted to Holy Orders, &c.—*Continued.*

Names.	Year of ordination.	Names.	Year of ordination.
Maud', Rev. G. J.	1858	† Ross, Rev. E. G. W.	1843
Manning, Rev. P. J.	1859	Ross, Rev. W. M.	1854
Merrick, Rev. W.	1849	Scarsing, Rev. H.	1837
Milne, Rev. G.	1841	Scott, Rev. J.	1843
Mitchell, Rev. R.	1861	Sewell, Rev. H. O.	1837
Morice, Rev. C.	1842	Simpson, Rev. J. E. F.	1844
† Mornbert, Rev. J. J.	1858	Simpson, Rev. S.	1848
† Morris, Rev. C. J.	1841	Slack, Rev. G.	1843
* Morris, Rev. E.	1859	Smith, Rev. F. A.	1856
Morris, Rev. W.	1842	Stephenson, Rev. R. E.	1850
Mountain, Rev. A. W.	1846	* Street, Rev. G. C.	1859
Mountain, Rev. J. J.	1847	† Strong, Rev. S. S.	1836
Nevs, Rev. F. S.	1843	Sutton, Rev. F. G.	1844
† O'Meara, Rev. F. A.	1838	Thompson, Rev. W.	1840
† Osler, Rev. F. L.	1837	Torrance, Rev. J.	1859
Parkin, Rev. E. C.	1844	† Usher, Rev. J. A.	1856
Parnther, Rev. D. B.	1840	† Vackoil, Rev. H.	1856
Pennyfather, Rev. T.	1857	Van Linge, Rev. J.	1849
* Petrie, Rev. G.	1859	Vial, Rev. W. S.	1859
Piers, Rev. R. G.	1841	* Von Iffland, Rev. A. A.	1862
Pyke, Rev. J.	1859	Waie, Rev. W. W.	1858
† Reed, Rev. C. P.	1856	* Ward, Rev. R. J.	1859
Reynolds, Rev. H. D.	1854	White, Rev. J. P.	1843
Richmond, Rev. J. P.	1860	Whitten, Rev. A.	1843
Richmond, Rev. W.	1860	Wickes, Rev. W.	1850
Roberts, Rev. C.	1861	Willoughby, Rev. M.	1859
Robinson, Rev. F.	1847	Woolrich, Rev. A. J.	1855
Robinson, Rev. W. B.	1842	Wurrele, Rev. L. O.	1859
Roe, Rev. H.	1852	* Young, Rev. J.	1848
Rollit, Rev. C.	1844	* Young, Rev. T. A.	1849

Those whose names are marked thus * were ordained Deacons only.

Those whose names are marked thus † were ordained Priests only.

Those whose names are unaccompanied by any indicative sign were ordained Deacons in the year mentioned, by the Bishop of Quebec, and Priests at a subsequent period.

THE HON. AND RIGHT REV.
JOHN STRACHAN, D.D., LL.D.,
FIRST BISHOP OF TORONTO.

The estimation and value of a man consists in the heart and in the will. There, his true honour lives. Valour is stability, not of legs and arms, but of the courage and the soul. It does not lie in the goodness of our horse, or of our arms, but in ourselves. He that falls, firm in his courage. "Si succiderit, de genu pugnat." "If his legs fail him, fights upon his knees," he, who despite the danger of death near at hand, abates nothing of his assurance; who, dying does yet dart at his enemy a fierce and disdainful look, is overcome, not by us, but by fortune; he is killed, not conquered; the most valiant are sometimes the most unfortunate. There are some defeats more triumphant than victories. * * * *The part that true conquering has to play lies in the encounter, not in the coming off. The honour of valour consists in fighting not in subduing.*—MONTAIGNE'S ESSAYS, COTTON'S TRANSLATION REVISED BY HAZLITT, EDITION 1845.

THE HON. AND RIGHT REV.
JOHN STRACHAN, D.D., LL.D.,

FIRST BISHOP OF TORONTO.

CHAPTER FIRST.

"I will tell you," said Lord Eldon to Mrs. Foster, referring to the election of the Duke of Wellington as Chancellor of the University of Oxford, "what charmed me very much when I left the theatre, and was trying to get into my carriage; one man in the crowd shouted out, 'There is old Eldon, cheer him, for he never ratted.' I was very much delighted, for I never did rat. I will not say I have been right through life. I may have been wrong. But I will say I have been consistent."—*Public and Private Life of Lord Chancellor Eldon; by Horace Twiss, Esq.*

FOR the same reason, there were very few persons in Canada who would not have given a cheer for the Bishop of Toronto. Not that they wholly disbelieved the story of his early leanings towards the Scotch establishment, or being Presbyterians, forgave his final preference for the English Church; not that they sympathized with the grandeur, or regretted the failure of his most cherished endeavours, but they remembered how consistent and free from guile those endeavours had been, with what ingenuousness and singleness of purpose he had laboured for what he had believed to be right; and how conspicuously such labours were marked with the sterling virtues of truth, courage, and endurance. People who disliked his style, and took exception to his manner, who could not concur with him in his opinions, or co-operate with him in his policy, nevertheless acknowledged the fascination of his character, and felt their hearts drawn with boyish sympathy towards him, not only because he "never ratted," but because, like a knight of a chivalrous order, he neither stooped to parley nor listened to compromise; neither calculated the forces that were opposed to him, nor counted the cost of defeat; but, indifferent alike to the odds or the issue, he closed fairly with the adversary, prepared if need be, to accept the loss of all things for a cause he was anxious to defend but not willing to betray. Though a vesture of humility, his cassock covered as brave a heart as ever beat beneath a breastplate; for he was in fact a "soldier" as well as a "servant of Christ's Church militant here upon earth;" the Church which, according to his belief, was by human law as well as by Divine appointment established in the land—the Church of his Sovereign and of his own choice, whose beneficent influence, like a goodly cedar tree, should in his judgment, be fostered with care, that it might overspread the land with blessing.

The minds and affections of generous men, irrespective of party, country, or creed, instinctively warm towards what is thorough in character and heroic in conduct, and hence, many who opposed him politically, and differed from him theologically, felt that human nature itself was exalted in his person; for whatever the peculiarities of his education, the infirmities of his judgment, or the errors of his opinion, he was a fair and courageous as well as a high minded and inflexible opponent. Men knew where to look for and where to find him. He took no tortuous course, for he detested all crooked ways. Like Henry of Navarre, he was distinguished by the colour in his crest, and by his place in the battle, and he never sullied the one or slunk from the other. For nearly three score years his banner flag was blazoned with the same scroll, and illumined with the same letters. Two words, *semper idem*, described his character. In the sentiment those words expressed, and the conduct they inspired, was to be found the key note of the complimentary cheer which soothed "old Eldon," and which, for the same reason, might have gladdened the heart of the Bishop of Toronto, for the Canadian Prelate, like the English Peer, had "never ratted."

Unfortunately we have no space for the detailed narrative of a historian. We can only find time for the condensed sketch of a reviewer. Such a disability will scarcely be regarded with regret, since it is generally known that another, and a more skilled hand, has undertaken to perfect what we have only been able to perform in part. It is, we rejoice to hear, currently stated that the late Bishop was a conscientious journalist, and a careful preserver of papers, and therefore that interesting as well as elaborate autobiographical notes and manuscripts of his own life and times may be supposed to exist. With access to such materials, Dr. Bethune, the present Bishop of Toronto, who has naturally and properly been charged with the duty, will be enabled to compile an interesting and instructive memoir of his predecessor in the See. Such a memoir should receive a more than common welcome, as it will possess a more than common value, for it will not only be a narrative coeval with the history of Upper Canada, but it will fully represent the calm, thoughtful, and mature observations of a very acute observer, of one, who, as a divine and a politician, as a teacher and a statesman, stands by himself, distinct and distinguishable in the gallery of Canadian worthies.

In a speech delivered by Dr. Strachan, on the sixth of March, 1828, and published at the request of the Legislative Council of Upper Canada, some particulars are furnished of his early history which have not always been accurately rendered by those who have spoken on the subject. We learn from Dr. Strachan's account of his parentage and youth that his father was a *non-juror*, and that his mother was a member of the Scottish Relief denomination, a religious body that had seceded from the Presbyterian Church of Scotland. The former died when the subject of this memoir was very young, and although he was separated from the latter by constraining circumstances at an early age, his religious principles were chiefly formed by and derived from her. It is therefore probable that such principles were more devout than argumentative, more hereditary than acquired. No doubt they were beautified with the purest of human examples, for they were entwined with the precepts and affections of the most tender and considerate of parents. They seem also to have been received without cavil or analysis and reverently applied by the son, for her sake, whose life they had adorned and beautified. Few have shewn more honour to the memory of their parents, than the Bishop of Toronto. When success crowned his efforts to establish a church university and he stood enclosed within circle of congratulation, he did not omit to state how much of that success was due to the lessons he acquired in humble life, and which were chiefly derived from the pious teachings of his mother. Perhaps the same might be said by the most of us, for the psalm of life generally derives its key note from the song of the cradle, and the saving grace of eternity is more or less associated with our earliest syllables in time. In his boyhood the Bishop sometimes accompanied his father to church, and sometimes he accompanied his mother to the meeting house. If we may credit a story that is still current in Presbyterian circles at Montreal, he was by no means impressed at that day with the beauty of the liturgal portions of what Sir Walter Scott calls "the suffering and Episcopal Church of Scotland," for he was accustomed to remark that "he did not care to go to church till read prayers were over." Whatever may have been the fluctuation of his thoughts or the inclination of his opinions on religious matters, they seemed not to have been governed by any historical considerations, or to have settled very steadily in any denominational direction, for when Dr. Strachan arrived in Canada, he had neither been confirmed by a bishop of his father's church, nor had he received the communion from a minister of his mother's church. In fact he had by no religious act of his own become a member of any religious body. Thus it would appear that while, on the one hand, Dr. Strachan on his own confession had deep religious feelings, on the other he shewed by his conduct that he had no well defined theological principles. The latter were an after growth, the result of clearer knowledge and closer study.

It may be observed that Episcopacy in Scotland was at that day, and to some extent is still, under a bann, for Prince Charles Edward, the heir of the Stuarts, then lived, nor was it until after his death, in 1788, that the old Episcopalians of that country, who, for the most part, were *non-jurants*, would read prayers for the reigning family of Hanover. Mr. Strachan's parents (the name, by the way, seems to have been derived from, and was probably a corruption of, Strathaen, or the "Valley of the Aen"), resided at Aberdeen, where he was born on the 12th April, 1778. The time is noteworthy, for it was two months after France had recognized the independence of the thirteen rebellious Provinces in America, and had promised the material aid which contributed mainly to bring that event about. The success of the rebellion was closely followed by the exile and dispersion of the North American Loyalists, and their partial settlement in Canada. Such men, representing the best blood of America, were among the earliest and most steadfast of those dear friends whom Mr. Strachan won and never lost. Their opinions, as well as their aversions, very materially influenced his, for, like them, he was a royalist, on whose broad brow, to use Colonel Coffin's[*] striking metaphor, the "Tower mark of Stirling was indelibly engraved." Like them, too, loyalty with him was a passion as well as a sentiment—a resolve as well as a duty. He cherished a monarchical and loathed a republican form of government; and subsequent observation only increased his admiration of the former and his aversion to the

[*] The War of 1812 and its moral; by W. F. Coffin.

latter. Could he have persuaded men to think as he came to think then would he have established "in every church a bishop, and in every state a king."

Though in narrow circumstances, and comparatively humble position, Mr. Strachan's father and mother were high-minded and sagacious people, thoroughly imbued with the national sentiment on the value of education, which they spared no pains to impress on the mind of their son. How earnestly, and under what difficulties that son followed their counsel, it were more easy to conjecture than to describe, more convenient to envy than to imitate. Without inquiring where he received his elementary education we learn that he obtained his A.M. degree at King's College, Aberdeen, in 1796, and that he then removed to the vicinity of St. Andrews, where he contracted several important and lasting friendships, amongst others, with the learned Thomas Duncan, afterwards Professor of Mathematics, and also with Dr. Chalmers, "since then so deservedly renowned." After leaving St. Andrews he was for a time employed in private tuition, but having a mother and two sisters in a great degree dependent on his exertion, he applied for the parochial school of Kettle, in the county of Fife, and obtained it by public competition.

This ordeal represented one of the turning points of his life. Small of stature, boyish in appearance, for the ruddy flush of youth had not forsaken his cheeks, and nineteen years of age, he found himself in a room, a competitor with forty-nine others, for the mastership of a parish school. The chances did not appear promising, but the indomitable pluck and perseverance, which befriended him through life, then assumed those forms of persistent resolve which so constantly shewed themselves in his career. With Lord Brougham, he seems to have regarded the word "impossible" as the mother tongue of little souls, for his determination of character was commonly expressed in the emphatic and well remembered words, uttered, we need scarcely add, in his much cherished but inimitable Aberdeen accent, which we can neither speak nor spell, "I never give up." He did not "give up," then. On the contrary, he seemed from the first to bend men and events to his will, and though he could not at all times command the success he then achieved, he at least made great efforts to deserve it. The examiners declared his to be the best papers, and him as a matter of course the successful candidate. When the stripling made his bow and claimed his prize, the elders who were assembled to bestow it, were dismayed at his youthful aspect. Indeed they would have re-considered the decision with a view to escape from its obligations, had not one of their number, a writer to the signet, shrewdly suggested that such a proceeding might expose them to the peril of a law suit; on that account, the lawyer suggested, it would be safer for themselves, as well as fairer to the lad, to keep to their contract; shrewdly adding, by way of solace, that should Mr. Strachan be found unequal to the duties they would be at liberty to dismiss him. Under such circumstances the young schoolmaster took his place as the teacher of one hundred and twenty-seven boys, some of whom were older and many were taller than himself.

Thus it was at the age of nineteen he commenced that career of educational labour in which he was destined to achieve very marked success. Among his pupils at Kettle was Sir David Wilkie, who, at the height of his career, had the candour to avow that he owed everything to his Reverend teacher. In fact Dr. Strachan was the first to perceive the genius of his pupil, and having made the discovery he spared no pains to give it the direction which eventually led to fame and to fortune. Commodore Robert Barclay, whose gallantry was as conspicuous as his misfortune on Lake Erie in the American war of 1812, was another of his pupils of whom he used to speak with warmth as well as pride. While at St. Andrews he attracted the notice and won the regard of the Rev. James Brown, one of the acting professors of the university, who was afterwards promoted to the chair of Natural Philosophy in the University of Glasgow. On removing to Glasgow the professor was anxious to secure Mr. Strachan's services and at the same time bring him into contact with the authorities of that university. To this end he proposed that Mr. Strachan should become his attending assistant to prepare and make the necessary experiments for the illustration of the professor's lectures, and in his absence to read those lectures, and generally to discharge such other college duties as he was competent to perform. But difficulties intervened which included the retirement of the professor, and thus a congenial career which opened unexpectedly was as unexpectedly closed. The disappointment was a bitter one, but it seems to have been the needful discipline through which the sufferer was to pass to honour and distinction. In the absence of such a trial it is probable that Dr. Strachan would not have accepted employment in Canada and would have missed the flood tide which was to " flow to fortune."

For three years before and during the time when Mr. Strachan was teaching the parish school at Kettle some noteworthy events were in progress in Canada which were destined to give shape to his opinions as well as to his career, but of which he then probably knew nothing. About ten thousand United Empire Loyalists had obtained the King's license to settle in the western portion of the old province of Quebec. For them, if not at their instance, that province was separated into the provinces of Upper and Lower Canada, with distinct governments and distinguishing laws. The thoughtful minds of England in church and state endeavoured to extract lessons of wisdom from adversity, and apply them anew to the vexed problem of colonial government in the infant province of Upper Canada. Unlike some of the older plantations in America which had been used as coverts for outlaws and penitentiaries for felons, Upper Canada, if not the chosen theatre of a poetical trust, was at all events the special allotment of a praiseworthy destiny. At the outset, the province was to be peopled by men on whose characters the soil of crime had not rested, by men whom virtue had ennobled, who had surrendered possessions for a sentiment, and had suffered the loss of all things in the cause of their prince and their flag. Neither were the king and parliament of that day disposed to regard such sacrifices with indifference; on the contrary, they honoured the weakness of a patriotic affection and did what they could to treat it with respect. Statesmen did not accustom themselves to sneer at the exuberant loyalty of the

Canadian people, or complain of being embarrassed by its demonstrative qualities. Dire experience had taught them that the absence of that sentiment in the old colonies had been followed by disaster, and that therefore the presence of it in the new ones should be fostered as the synonym of safety. Thus was it that an exuberant loyalty was not only tolerated as a passion, but it was treated as a virtue. To utilize such loyalty and give stability to the monarchical principle which it represented, the constitutional act, as it was termed, was passed, and His Excellency Major-General Simcoe, the first Lieutenant-Governor of Upper Canada, was charged with the duty of giving force to its provisions.

In his opening speech to the Parliament of Upper Canada, made at Newark, now Niagara, on the 17th September, 1792, His Excellency amongst other things said:

> I have summoned you together under the authority of an Act of the Parliament of Great Britain passed in the last year, and which has established the British Constitution, and also the forms which secure and maintain it, in this distant country. The wisdom and beneficence of our Most Gracious Sovereign and the British Parliament, have been eminently proved, not only in imparting to us the same form of government, but also in securing the benefit of the many provisions that guard this memorable act, so that the blessings of our invaluable Constitution, thus protected and amplified, we hope will be extended to the remotest posterity.

In closing the same session, on the 15th of the following month, His Excellency said:

> I cannot dismiss you without earnestly desiring you to promote, by precept and example, among your respective counties, the regular habits of piety and morality, the surest

foundations of all private and public felicity; and at this juncture I particularly recommend to you to explain that this Province is singularly blessed, not with a mutilated Constitution, but with a Constitution which has stood the test of experience, and is the very image and transcript of that of Great Britain, by which she has long established and secured to her subjects as much freedom and happiness as is possible to be enjoyed under the subordination necessary to civilized society.

In 1793, the two provinces of Upper and Lower Canada were erected into a distinct See, and on All Saints day, the first of November of that year, the Right Reverend Jacob Mountain, D.D., arrived in Canada, having previously been created Bishop of Quebec. In 1795, that Prelate was summoned to the Executive and Legislative Councils of Lower Canada, and on the 25th January, 1796, Lord Dorchester advised Governor Simcoe, that His Majesty had been pleased, under royal mandamus, to appoint "the Right Reverend Father in God, Jacob, Bishop of Quebec and its dependencies, to be of the Executive Council in the Province of Upper Canada." No special explanation accompanied the order, but the student of English constitutional history will have little difficulty in discovering a reason for the proceeding in the analogous practice of the mother country, where the senior Bishop of England, who is, of course, the Archbishop of Canterbury, by ancient and prescriptive right is entitled to be present at all meetings of the Privy Council, irrespective of the consideration whether such meetings are confidential or otherwise. It is therefore probable that the authors of the Act of 1791, as well as those who were commissioned to carry out its provisions, were desirous that the spiritual element should not be absent from a form of government which was said to be "the very image and transcript of that of Great Britain."

To make the constitution symmetrical, if not perfect, in its resemblance, the missing part was supplied, and hence it came about that the church and state in Canada, as in England, were represented in the same government. This practical commentary, taken in connection with the words of the constitutional act, with the words of the coronation oath, and with the debates which took place in Parliament at the time, gave colour to their opinions, who asserted that the "very image and transcript" of the British Constitution included the church of England as truly as it did the law of England. How far such opinions were accurate, is no part of our business to inquire, but such, and kindred incidents should be steadily borne in mind, if we would fairly appreciate the character and conduct of the late Bishop of Toronto; for the faults of his life, and the fame of his life, are in no small degree traceable to the interpretation he attached to those incidents.

On the 20th July, 1796, Governor Simcoe, in a despatch to the Duke of Portland, recommended that the sevenths of the Crown lands should be sold for Public purposes, "the first and chief of which I beg to offer with all respect and deference to your Grace, must be the erection and endowment of an University from which more than from any other service or circumstance whatsoever, a grateful attachment to His Majesty's government, morality and religion will be fostered, and take root throughout the whole Province."

We have no means of knowing what answer was returned to the foregoing recommendation, but that it was favourably entertained we may fairly assume from the following passage of the Bishop's narrative:

> Among the many schemes contemplated by General Simcoe, for the benefit of the province, was that of establishing Grammar schools in every district, and a University at their head, at the seat of Government.
>
> Anxious to complete, as soon as possible, so beneficial an object, the Governor gave authority to the late Hon. Richard Cartwright and the Hon. Robert Hamilton, to procure a gentleman from Scotland to organize and take charge of such College or University. These gentlemen, whose memories are still dear to the province, applied to their friends in St. Andrews, who offered the appointment first to Mr. Duncan, then to Mr. Chalmers, neither of whom were yet much known, but both declined. Overtures were then made to me, and, suffering severely under my recent disappointment, I was induced after some hesitation to accept the appointment.

Mr. Strachan sailed from Greenock towards the end of August, 1799, under convoy, but, from various causes, he did not reach Kingston until the last day of that year. Fatigued and disappointed in body and mind, he was made more miserable by learning that Governor Simcoe had returned to England, and that the establishment of the University which he had projected had been indefinitely postponed. Nevertheless, as in a former crisis of his history, misfortune again befriended one who seemed born to be fortunate. "Had I possessed the means," the Bishop, in after life, told his clergy, "I should at once have returned to Scotland." But not having the means of gratifying his desire, he resolutely, and with a cheerful mind, endeavoured to discharge his duty. Instead of being the principal of a college he accepted the situation of private tutor to a family, and by doing so he not only won for himself the means of present support, but he found the opportunity of forming and settling his religious opinions on a foundation satisfactory to his reason and consoling to his heart. At the invitation of Mr. Cartwright, of Kingston, in whose house Mr. Strachan resided for three years, and under the guidance of the Rev. Dr. Stuart, the Rector of the town, he studied divinity with a view to taking orders in the Church of England. Accordingly, on the second of May, 1803, he was admitted by Dr. Mountain, the first Protestant Bishop of Quebec, to the order of Deacon, and on the third of June in the following year, to the order of Priest, and forthwith appointed to the mission of Cornwall. In addition to missionary labour, and at the request of some of the parents of those who had been his pupils at Kingston, he determined to continue the work of tuition, and hence the establishment of the Cornwall school, which, under his direction, was destined to rise into local celebrity.

Clergymen often observe what indeed laymen have much reason to notice that what are termed distinctive church principles were less dwelt on seventy years ago than they are now; and this fact being connected with the common belief at the time, that the Church of England was established by law in Canada, may have done much towards giving the direction which Mr. Strachan's ecclesiastical career was destined to take. Another point should also be noted as among the common errors of the period. "The Church," and "the Establishment," the spiritual body, and the political fabric, were spoken of indifferently, as if people were unaccustomed to distinguish any variance in the terms; thus Lord Chancellor Eldon, for example, as well as many of his contemporaries, were in the habit of calling themselves members of "the Establishment." In like manner old fashioned members of the Church of Scotland qualified, so to speak, as members of "the Establishment" in that part of the kingdom, and, moreover, they had an intense repugnance to being accounted dissenters. Rather than incur such contumely or take their station in the outer court when they might stand within the temple itself, it was by no means an unusual circumstance for a Scotsman resident in England to conform to the established church of England, because it represented "the Establishment." A native of Dundee, resident in London, said in the hearing of the writer: "I like my religion to rest upon a law basis. In Scotland I go to the established church, and in England I go to the established church, and for the same reason in both countries because they are established." In like manner an Aberdeen immigrant settled in Canada might not have been insensible to similar considerations. If such an one intended to take holy orders he would not, at that day, have been indifferent to the important contingency whether by so doing he would become a minister of a church "by law established," or a preacher of a sect by custom tolerated. Change of opinion, if it really took place, formed no exception in the case of Mr. Strachan to the rule which commonly governs all such changes; that is to say, it was gradual but progressive, unobtrusive but continuous, where controversy was rather avoided than sought for, and conviction, like conversion, was a process rather than a surprise. Luther, at the outset of his career, made but slow progress towards those opinions which rendered his later life illustrious, nevertheless the fact that he had but partially ascertained the ground work of his new opinions did not prevent his building in what he had ascertained. Doctrinal disquisitions were then, more generally than they are now, regarded by English people as the especial property of the spiritual order with which the laity had but little to do. Read by the light of some contemporary memoirs, such exercises seem to have been regarded as theological gymnastics, possibly requisite for the mental health of the clergy, but of no moral worth to the generality of the laity. Simple country folk declined to disquiet themselves with subtleties; they were content according to their capacity to believe those things which a christian ought to know, and they illustrated their belief by the duty of "holy living" as the prime requisite to "holy dying." Moreover the earnest men of that day were called upon to engage in other controversies than those which turned on distinguishing Church principles. They had to take up the challenge of infidelity, and wrestle with the aggressive forms of unbelief which showed themselves at the end of the last and at the beginning of the present century. This duty with respect to a common danger had a tendency to bring together the religious elements of the community, and to unite them for certain purposes in the bonds of a conventional brotherhood. Thus the settlers in Canada, whether Episcopalians or Presbyterians, learned to respect one another, and many of them, having in the spirit of gentleness, rather than of controversy, compared notes, began to see the common advantage of ecclesiastical union, and from that time some of the latter became earnest members of the Anglican Church.

The Venerable Archdeacon Fuller, in a sermon preached on the occasion of the Bishop's death at St. George's Church, Toronto, on the 10th of November, 1867, says: "Having the charge of the Parish of Cornwall he (the Bishop) had to visit a good deal among his parishioners, besides having to prepare his sermons for Sunday. He had also to study every night quite as hard as the boys, 'for I was not,' as the Bishop elsewhere observed of himself, 'much in advance of the highest class in school. Those duties demanded sixteen hours every day, and yet those nine years were the happiest years of my life.' To be sure, the nine years included an event of personal interest, the prospect of which very commonly exerts an exhilarating influence on the minds, and the realization of which is not unattended with important results to the estates of men. The young clergyman's conduct was worthy, alike of praise and of imitation, for if there be truth in local traditions he shewed his taste by marrying the prettiest, his prudence by marrying the richest, and his good judgment by marrying one of the nicest young gentlewomen in the old town of Cornwall. The event took place in 1807, and the lady was Ann, a daughter of George Thomson Wood, Esq., M.D., a retired surgeon of the army, and the relict of James McGill, Esq., a wealthy and influential resident of that town, by whom the Bishop had a numerous family. Mrs. Strachan died only a year or two before the Bishop. In the year, 1807, the degree of LL.D. was conferred on him by the University of St. Andrews, and that of D.D. by the University of Aberdeen. Though we anticipate the course of our narrative, we may here note that in 1812, he was appointed

Rector of York; in 1827, Archdeacon of York; and in 1839, Bishop of Toronto.

The Cornwall school, and subsequently the York or Toronto school, under the same astute master, became notable schools. All who desired for their sons a sound education from a Protestant teacher, and could afford the expense, sent them to the Rev. John Strachan, D.D. The roll of the scholars of those schools who were living in the year 1828,* included the names of the greater number of the foremost men of Canada. Men who did credit not only to the teachings, but to the character, as well as the principles of their teacher. Of those scholars few survive.—The "oldest boy" is probably the present Dean of Montreal, now upwards of eighty years of age. His veneration for his old master has known neither change nor abatement, and it was a pleasing sight to see the two dignitaries, a few years since, walking arm in arm within the Cathedral Close of Montreal, for it showed that the wine of friendship had not spoiled by age.

The period of his residence at Cornwall was not only the happiest, it was especially the poetic period of the Bishop's life. We have been informed that he was a facile writer of verse, and that some of his poetical compositions in the form of odes and songs are still extant. The Dean of Montreal, in a letter lately addressed by him to the writer, observes: "the Bishop certainly wrote quite a number of fugitive pieces, such as prologues and epilogues, for his

* See Appendix No. 1, to this sketch.

annual school exhibitions; also, prose pieces and even debates for the same occasions." But though a ready rhymer and a lover of song, Mr. Strachan was not suspected of a very intimate acquaintance with music. It was for example his constant habit in a low soothing way to whistle as he walked, but like the droning of an imbecile bagpipe, or of a sleepy child, his notes indicated rather a tuneless sense of happiness than a tuneful expression of melody. Some people persuaded themselves that they could detect in those notes the air of a familiar song, but we incline to think they knew as little of the tune which they affected to be acquainted with, as the Bishop did of the words to which it was set. It is one thing to write songs and another to sing them; for poets are not necessarily musicians. That he wrote the former we have little doubt, but we have never heard that he attempted the latter. Indeed his general character discourages such belief, for it was not his habit to undertake what he had not the ability to perform.

A new page in his life was about to open. The war of 1812 had broken out. That heroic soldier, Major General Sir Isaac Brock, not only had a bold man's appreciation of a brave man, but he also possessed a statesman's perception of a useful man. There was a dearth of intellectual culture in the country at the time for there were few persons who had enjoyed the advantage of an education equal to that which was imparted at the Cornwall school; therefore the master of that school, though neither a very learned man nor a very ripe scholar, was by comparison and in virtue of his position looked upon as a kind of local encyclopedia of wisdom and culture. It is true that soldiers were chiefly necessary, but the General was not unaware of the fact that the sword could be sharpened with the pen, and that a good cause might be greatly aided by a good commentator, by one who, like a minstrel of the earlier days, could stir the hearts through the minds of men. Hence, at the instance of Major General Sir Isaac Brock, Dr. Strachan was transferred from Cornwall to Toronto in succession to his friend, Mr. Stuart, who was appointed to the town of Kingston. The qualities of pluck and resoluteness which distinguished the former through life, received more than one illustration during the continuance, and after the close of the war. Archdeacon Fuller mentions that Dr. Strachan's journey to Toronto was marked with the following amusing incident:

"On his way up the St. Lawrence in a small vessel, which contained his family and all his worldly goods, the courage of the late Bishop was put to the test. A vessel hove in sight, which the Captain supposed to be an American armed schooner, and it being during the war with the United States, he became alarmed, and came down to Dr. Strachan into the little cabin, and consulted with him about surrendering his craft to the enemy. The Doctor enquired of him if he had any means of defence, and ascertaining that he had a fourpounder and a few muskets on board, he insisted on the Captain defending his vessel; but to no purpose, as he was entirely overcome by fear. The Doctor finding that he could not induce the captain to defend his vessel, told him to intrust the defence of it to him, and to stay with his family in the cabin. This proposition was gladly acceded to by the Captain. Whereupon the future Bishop mounted "the companion way" fully determined to defend the little craft to the utmost of his power, but (as he remarked when detailing this incident to me some years ago,) "fortunately for me, the schooner bearing down upon us proved to be a Canadian schooner —not an American—for the four-pounder was fastened to the deck, and it pointed to the starboard, whereas the schooner came to us on the larboard bow!"

Second Chapter.

My opinion is that the Establishment is secured, not for the purpose of making the church political, but for the purpose of making the state religious.—Keble.

Public and Private Life of Lord Chancellor Eldon; by Horace Twiss, Esq.

ON arriving at Toronto, the new Rector laid himself out for work, and it was such work as the dangerous times and a beleaguered Province laid upon brave and patriotic men, whether clerical or lay. In the furtherance of such work, Dr. Strachan made plans for and was chiefly instrumental in establishing "The loyal and patriotic society," and for many years was its chief almoner. This charitable institution, it was said, did as much towards the defence of the Province as half a dozen regiments. At the battle of York, the "little Rector" seems to have combined the characters of priest, soldier and diplomatist. As a clergyman, he ministered to the wants of the wounded, and prayed with the dying. As a soldier, he prevented plunder and recovered spoil, and as a diplomatist, he did much towards saving the town from sack and violence. Without dwelling upon the sacred duties of his profession, we may mention one incident that will illustrate his coolness, and another that will show his tact. The Honourable George Boulton, a very young volunteer of that day, mentioned to him that two American soldiers, fully armed, had visited the house of Colonel Givens, a British officer, at that time with the retreating army. Having menaced the unprotected occupants of the isolated dwelling, the soldiers coolly helped themselves to what "loot" they could conveniently carry away, including a silver tea-pot, which they secreted with other valuables, about their persons. Acting under the conviction that skulkers were cowards, Dr. Strachan boldly advanced towards them and demanded their ill-gotten spoil. They answered the challenge by leveling their muskets at the gallant little clergyman. Nothing daunted, the latter stood his ground, and reiterated in bolder language, his demand for the restoration of their plunder. In such strangely contrasted styles, and with such different weapons, the soldiers and the priest confronted one another; and the question whether moral or material force would triumph, was still undecided, when, through the vigilance of the volunteer already mentioned, a valuable ally was brought to the rescue, in the person of an American officer, who at once put an end to a nervous pantomime, by ordering the soldiers to surrender their booty. Again when the garrison magazine was exploded, and with fatal effect to General Pike and a considerable portion of the invading force, General Dearborn was not unnaturally exasperated, and threatened to revenge the sacrifice of his soldiers on the unoffending inhabitants of the town, by burning it to the ground. Hearing that such intentions were entertained, the magistrates deputed Dr. Strachan to invite the General to a parley. We shall quote the words of another:

"His great firmness of character saved the town of York, in 1813, from sharing the same fate as the town of Niagara met with some months afterwards. The American General Pike having attacked and routed the small force defending York, was shortly after killed by the blowing up of the magazine in the garrison. His successor, being enraged by the incident, though it was not attributable to any of the inhabitants of the town, determined to have vengeance on them and to burn down the town. This determination coming to the knowledge of the authorities, they deputed Dr. Strachan to remonstrate with the American Commander (General Dearborn) against this intended act of barbarity. He met him in the old fort; and I have been told by men who witnessed the interview between these parties, that words ran high between them; the American General declaring that he would burn the town, and the future Bishop declaring that if he persisted in his atrocious act of barbarity, vengeance would be taken upon the Americans for such an unheard of outrage; and that Buffalo, Lewiston, Sackett's Harbour, and Oswego would in course of time (as soon as troops could be brought from England) share its fate. The earnestness and determination of Dr. Strachan moved the General from his barbarous purpose, and York was saved from the flames."

The war and its perils had given a well-merited celebrity to the services which Dr. Strachan had been able to render, for he had shewn himself to be wise in counsel and courageous in action. It was, therefore, natural enough that the sagacious display of such qualities should have inclined men to think well of and place confidence in him. Thus the favourable impressions which had been privately formed of his conduct and capacity were publicly confirmed when the convenient season arrived, for he suddenly found himself menaced with the calamity of those of whom all men speak well. So far as we are informed, there is no evidence whatever to shew that he then aspired to the political prominence which he afterwards obtained. On the other hand, it can scarcely be questioned that he had been brought into positions perilous to his subsequent peace. He had entered the delectable land, where the thirst for rule is more easily acquired than quenched, where the mind becomes excited with its own portraitures, and irrepressible aspirations involuntarily arise from the newly-awakened passion for power. Such a passion is no slavish lust, though, in the intensity of its character, it may resemble less elevated desires. On the contrary, it is noble in its aim, for such aim is nothing less than to give shape and vitality to those plans of virtue and purposes of good which the irresistible will deems to be worthy of immediate attainment. Thus, it not unfrequently happens, that a duty which a passing accident has imposed, becomes an obligation from which there is no possibility of escape. For example, Dr. Strachan's connection with public affairs was not of his seeking. It arose out of the exigences of the times, and especially from the menaced and imperilled state of the Province. The continuance of his connection with those affairs must be regarded as the logical sequence of an accident, for the difficulties of government did not disappear with a return of peace. On the contrary, when the enemy had withdrawn within his own frontier, the high-spirited people whom he had ruined, and the noble province he had ravaged, had to be ruled, and men of approved sagacity were required for that purpose. The services which Dr. Strachan had rendered were neither unknown nor unappreciated, and being alike popular and useful, the loyal men of Canada found little difficulty in determining that he who had proved equal to the duty of serving them by his wisdom in a time of danger, would be equal to the duty of serving them by his counsel, in the time of safety. Moreover, the fact that Dr. Strachan was a clergyman, may have been, and probably was, regarded by many as an advantage rather than a drawback. At all events, it was not deemed to be a disqualification. The constitution of Upper Canada had theretofore failed in one important respect to resemble the constitution of England, of which it was said to be the "image and transcript." The missing element was the church, for until then the state only had been represented in the Upper House of the Legislature. Again, the war of 1812, like the war of the revolution, which ended in the independence of the American Provinces, had caused the people of Upper Canada to compare their own political system with the system of government which obtained in England, and if possible to make a closer approximation to uniformity between the practice they had followed and the practice they were anxious to follow—to inquire wherein the analogy was incomplete, and to take measures to supply what was wanting. That a connection of some kind between church and state in Upper Canada was supposed to exist, may be gathered from the circumstances already mentioned. Governor Simcoe, the first representative of the Sovereign in the newly created Province of Upper Canada, had in effect if not in words told the people through their representatives in the Legislature that such was the case, and by way of corroboration the first Anglican Bishop of Quebec, on his arrival was appointed, by Royal command, to be a member of the Executive Council of that Province. The appointment seems to have been *ex officio* only, for there is not, so far as we can discover, any record of that prelate having taken his seat. After the war was ended, it is probable that the question, which had been theoretically met in the way we have mentioned, came up again in a practical form, and with such force as to demand an exact solution. There was no Bishop in Upper Canada upon whom to confer political distinction, and it may, on that account, have been thought desirable that the most eligible clergyman should be chosen to represent the sacred part in a government which was to include both the temporal and the spiritual orders, since it was to be the counterpart of the constitution of the parent State.

Such aims were probably as congenial to the mind of Dr. Strachan, as they possibly were at that day to the people among whom his lot had been cast. But in applying those aims a path of life was opened before him for which he had in no wise prepared himself, and wherein to walk steadily would tax his efforts to the utmost, since statecraft and Christianity do not always walk hand in hand. In leaving his native land his ambition was circumscribed within the four imaginary walls of a newly formed university. But the university which he had supposed would be ready to receive him, was only dreamed of when he arrived; it was not planned, much less built. "No thoroughfare" was legibly written across his path. In a spirit of bitter disappointment he had to turn aside, but, as it chanced, to find a wider field of exertion and a greater space for usefulness. With reverence we may say, "that it is not in man that walketh to direct his steps." A plan of life appeared to be appointed for him by hands other than his own, for a singular combination of fortuitous accidents, like swathing bands divinely wrought, seemed to enclose him as with a girdle. He may have drawn a long anxious breath as he weighed his duties and his responsibilities, for in conforming to the obligations they entailed, he sacrificed ease and peace to irksome toil and, as the result proved, to untiring opposition. No doubt he intended to serve the Church by accepting service in the state, for he wished by the official contact of the former with the latter to increase the influence and add to the beauty of religion. And though it may be questioned whether means so alien to peace did not do much towards frustrating the end they were designed to serve, still it should be borne in mind that in obeying the command of his sovereign to take part in the counsels of the state, he was only seeking to perfect the similitude between the Upper House of the Province, and the Upper House of the Empire, and moreover, that he was doing so in the way most persons at that day were inclined to regard as the right way, for the Mandamus by which Legislative Councillors were then summoned to the Upper House, was expressed in these words: " Know ye, that as well for the especial trust and confidence we have manifested in you as for the purpose of obtaining your advice and assistance in all weighty and arduous affairs, which may the state and defence of our Province of Canada, and the Church thereof concern," &c. It is probable that Dr. Strachan, and many others at that day in Upper Canada placed a too literal interpretation on the somewhat vague phraseology of the King's writ, and consequently that his deductions therefrom were somewhat exaggerated in their form and went beyond the terms of any statute then existent relating to Canada. Nevertheless the words of that writ, and the inferences which those words encouraged, may very fairly have excused him for regarding himself as the especial champion and representative of the church, in the state. The honour, in whatever light regarded, was necessarily associated with duties of a peculiar kind, for they were religious as well as political. The former could not very properly be overlooked by a clergyman, and the latter ought not to be avoided by any one who accepts service in the state. Dr. Strachan determined neither to omit nor evade them. How thoroughly the church of his choice had become the church of his affections is written in almost every page of his published works. How ardently he desired "to lengthen her cords and to strengthen her stakes," is seen in almost every effort of his active life. He neither questioned nor doubted the human blessedness of her office. He believed that the union between the church and the state which existed in the old country, ought not to be put asunder in Canada, for with the Earl of Eldon he was of opinion "that the Establishment is formed, not for the purpose of making the church political, but for the purpose of making the state religious."

The desire lay near his heart to make Canada resemble England, resemble her in religion, in manners, in character, in institutions and in laws. To this end he sought to establish rectories in stated places, to cover the Province with a net work of parishes, and to establish in each parish a centre of religious and educational influence, as well as of social and intellectual refinement. The picture of the future, which his fancy sketched, may have resembled the actual picture which Cobbett saw from one of the glorious uplands of his native county, and which, he has vividly described in his nervous writings. In imagination, Dr. Strachan beheld a noble Province, divided into parallelograms and apportioned into parishes, each parish the centre of an accredited representative of that genial, charitable and liberal christianity which is popularly associated with the national church. He wished that every parish should be the settled abode of a well educated, well mannered parson, whose character would be respected, and whose influence would be seen, in the every day intercourse of common life. His desire was that religion and learning should re-act on one another, that they should sanctify taste, elevate morals, purify manners and blend with the hard and roughening influences of the backwoods, many of the social refinements and home attractions which grow around the old grey church towers and add beauty to the trim parsonages of England. The machinery of church work through the whole of its educational course, from the cradle to the grave, formed in his mind a vision of present loveliness and future peace. Moreover he wished to unite and consolidate the Protestant forces of Upper Canada and thus create, under the protection of Canterbury, a power sufficiently venerable, and instructed to challenge the authority, to contest the arguments, and to resist the encroachments of the Church of Rome. To make the ideal real, he gave his mind to thought, and his life to toil. But alas! like the gourd of Jonah, the picture that Dr. Strachan painted of the parochial system in Canada, was as evanescent as it was beautiful, as perishable as it was fair, for he had no sooner taken his seat in the Council than the first shock of that moral earthquake was felt which ere long was to destroy the fabric which his fancy had fashioned, and leave amidst the debris, "leaded" as it were "in the rock," the old imperishable words "vanity of vanities, all is vanity."

Under an absolute form of administration, the qualities that marked the Bishop's character would probably have been turned to noteworthy account. In ordinary affairs he was inclined to sacrifice very little to sentiment, yet, on the subjects of morals and government, his enthusiasm bordered on the fanatical. Like his persistent antagonist, the late Honourable William Morris, the Canadian leader of the anti-clergy reserves party, Dr. Strachan was endowed, to a remarkable extent, with the Scottish qualities of tenacity and fortitude, with industry and perseverance, for he "never gave up." He was unswerving in endeavour, fertile in expedient, bold, self-reliant, and courageous. No perils deterred him, and no disappointments overcame him. His views on the subjects of enterprize and local improvement were large and statesmanlike. Indeed we have reliable testimony on this subject in the fact that the late Honourable W. H. Merritt's great plans for Western Extension via the Welland Canal, was from the first appreciated, and warmly supported by the Bishop. Nevertheless his political principles were too immobile to be in accord with the progressive age in which he lived, and with the institutions of the Province which he ruled. Apparently he had a supreme contempt for the class of politicians, who like weathercocks seem always to be waiting for the wind; hence he paid little attention to the current of public opinion or to the rise and fall of the popular pulse, and therefore he seemed incapable of appreciating, in their initial character, those menacing forms of thought which gradually arose to influence, and in the end to controul the course of events. In matters of political economy he was not disposed to be an advanced thinker, and he not unfrequently distrusted the revelations because he would not accept the deductions of science. As a public man he was disinclined to recognize the causes that produce a crisis in political affairs, or to foreshadow the consequences that may be expected to flow from them. Less gifted men, who ventured on such treacherous ground, were treated either with scorn, or with silence, and thus they were too often exasperated by the Bishop's prejudice, or made enemies by his contempt. He knew better how to resist than how to conciliate, how to face his opponent than how to take him in flank. He would not retreat that he might advance or overcome his adversary by giving ground. He was determined to win in his own way, or not to win at all. He was no adept in that species of statecraft which governs by dividing the forces of an opponent, which deranges the order of battle before the enemy has matured his plans, or consolidated his power. Matters of principle did not, in the Bishop's opinion, admit of conditions, and hence he was always ready to contend for what he believed to be "pure," being comparatively indifferent whether the strife was peaceful or the reverse. He fondled a prejudice with as much affection as he cherished a right, and sometimes claimed for a traditional conceit as much respect as for the lessons of experience. There was little moderation in his character, and, on matters theological, less generosity.

Throughout the earlier portion of his life he had absolutely ruled boys, and in his maturer years he had been required conditionally to govern men. This double obligation had given tenacity to the strength of his will, and stimulated the form of its expression. He had been accustomed to direct, and not to argue, and when accident imposed the latter duty upon him he seemed occasionally to be seized with a sensation of surprise, apparently, because his opinions were questioned, or his judgment doubted. It seldom occurred to him that he might be right only in part, and he rarely doubted that those who opposed him were altogether wrong. He acted vehemently, after the manner of a churchman who has a text to unfold, or a dogma to enforce, and not prudently after the manner of a statesman who has human beings to govern, and opposing interests to reconcile. It is true, indeed, that he kept his friends, but it is we fear equally true that he exasperated his opponents. "Strive for the truth unto death, and the Lord shall fight for thee," are the words of wisdom. It was, as the Bishop believed, "for the truth, the whole truth and nothing but the truth," that he struggled from first to last, and we have little doubt that he would have died rather than abate one jot, or surrender one tittle, of what he believed to be true.

We do not, in this short paper, intend to dwell at any length on, much less to consider critically, the public career of the late Bishop; that will be more ably and more fully done by his gifted successor in the See; but it may, nevertheless, be of interest to some, if we extract from the Parliamentary Papers of England, the first official expression of doubt that we can find as to the meaning of the words "Protestant

Clergy," accompanied, as it was, with the earliest effort, of which any record has been preserved, to open the clergy reserve question and assail the clergy reserve properties.

On the 17th of May, 1819, Sir Peregrine Maitland addressed a despatch to Earl Bathurst, the Secretary of State for the Colonies, with a petition from the Presbyterian inhabitants of the town of Niagara and its vicinity, praying for a yearly grant of £100 towards the support of a minister of the Church of Scotland, the patronage and selection being offered to the Lieutenant Governor. The petitioners suggested that the sum referred to "should be paid out of the money annually collected on account of Clergy Reserves." This petition, His Excellency observed, "involves a question on which I perceive there is a difference of opinion, viz.: Whether the act intends to extend the benefit of the reserves for the maintenance of a Protestant Clergy to all denominations, or only to those of the Church of England. The Law Officers seem to incline to the latter opinion." It will be observed that His Excellency had been advised to state the case in a very loose, not to say unfair way, for the question then raised was not between the "Church of England" and "all denominations," but between the Church of England and the Church of Scotland. The effort on the part of the friends of the former church to place the members of the latter in the category of dissenters was exceedingly injudicious, and helped to embitter the controversy that followed. To questions of law and divinity there were thus added elements of discourtesy, which were necessarily attended with a good deal of hard feeling as well as with very embarrassing consequences, consequences that were by no means qualified by the fact that the disputants, for the most part, were resolute and hard-headed Scotsmen who might tolerate equals, but who would not brook superiors. In his despatch, dated 20th May, 1820, in answer to the foregoing, Earl Bathurst noted the distinction which Sir Peregrine Maitland had failed to make.

His Lordship observed, "as to the right of Dissenting Protestant Ministers resident in Canada to partake of the lands directed by the Act 31 Geo. III, chap. 31, to be reserved as a provision for the support and maintenance of a Protestant Clergy, I have now to acquaint you that His Majesty's Law Officers are of opinion that though the provisions made by the 31 Geo. III, chap. 31, ss. 36 and 42, for the support and maintenance of a Protestant Clergy, are not confined solely to the Church of England, but may be extended also to the Clergy of the Church of Scotland, yet that they do not extend to Dissenting Ministers, since the terms "Protestant Clergy" can apply only to the Protestant Clergy recognized and established by law."

The distinction thus made by Earl Bathurst included results which would have proved fatal to Dr. Strachan's fond conceit of an establishment and of his cherished plan for creating one state church in Canada. Wherefore the Doctor, and those who thought with him, in an evil hour for the cause they desired to serve, determined to answer Earl Bathurst's *dictum* with a remonstrance.

The paper, which purports to be a "Petition of the Corporation for superintending, managing and conducting the Clergy Reserves within the Province of Upper Canada," is signed by John Strachan, D.D., as Chairman, and dated York, 22nd April, 1823. It is interesting, for it is written by one who understood the executive machinery of both Churches. It is also instructive, for it shows how little the course of general history is influenced by speculative opinion, and how commonly men fall into mistakes who overlook or make light of those powers which have their roots in ignorance as well as in learning, in envy as well as in good will. Prejudice is a power as well as knowledge. Vice is a power as well as virtue. Statesmen must not overlook such powers, for they exert wonderful influences in the Political government of communities as well as in the moral welfare of states. Without dwelling on such considerations, we shall only extract the concluding paragraph of the petition:

"That your Lordships' petitioners will not presume to state to your Lordships the strong feeling which they entertain of the irregularity and inexpediency of introducing at this day a new religious establishment in the Diocese of Quebec, and Province of Canterbury, but they are impelled by a sense of duty most earnestly, though most respectfully, to deprecate the rivalry to the Church of England, and those endless evils of disunion, competition and irritation of which a compliance with the Ministers of the Kirk of Scotland cannot fail, in the opinion of your Lordships' petitioners, most widely to scatter the seeds. They deprecate the erection of a particular interest to strengthen prejudices which may exist against the establishment not otherwise insuperable, to alienate minds which are neutral and undecided from conformity to the Church, and by so doing cut away one of the surest and safest bands which might connect them with the state. They deprecate the extinction of that hope of religious unanimity, in the future generations of Protestants, who shall occupy these fine and extensive countries, which can only be fostered and matured under the blessing of Divine Providence, by the judicious protection of the English Church establishment already formed, and the completion of the plan already provided by the wisdom of Government."

In 1818 Dr. Strachan was appointed a member of the Executive and Legislative Councils, and his connection continued with the former until 1836, and with the latter until the union of the Provinces in 1841. From the first mentioned year until 1854, when the clergy reserves were finally sequestrated, Dr. Strachan courageously fought his cause. Even when it was lost in the estimation of his supporters, and when compromise was advisable as well as possible, he still declined to be a party to what he believed was politically a great evil, and morally a great sin. Like one of old he regarded not the consequences, but refused to acquiesce in measures that had the taint and flavour of sacrilege. He left to those who chose to assume the responsibility, the work of appropriating to secular uses what had solemnly been set apart for sacred ones. It is not difficult to see the hand of Dr. Strachan in the despatches addressed by successive Lieutenant Governors to successive Colonial Secretaries. There are passages of irony almost bordering on banter in some of those documents, difficult even now to read without a smile—a smile that would be relishing could it be separated from the subject that provoked it. But though the struggle of thirty years ended in the defeat of the church party, that defeat was neither attended with disgrace nor followed by ill will. Even now, as the question is dispassionately considered, there are not a few among the victors who speak of their triumph as an injury to the principles of the reformation, and on that account would willingly have their places in history reversed, and thus go down to posterity side by side with the fine old Protestant churchman who "never ratted," but bravely fought his cause to the last.

Second only in importance to his effort to establish the Anglican Church in Upper Canada, and to secure to her in perpetuity what he at least regarded as her rightful patrimony, must be ranked his exertions for half a century to erect and endow a university on the model of the ancient universities of England. But his labours in this, as in the matters already mentioned, were destined to end in disappointment. It is true indeed that the existence of the University of Toronto, as well as of the Upper Canada College, are indirectly due to his exertions; for in procuring a charter for the predecessor of the first named institution he laid the foundation of the present University. But though he is fairly referred to in the language of compliment as its founder, nevertheless the honour so far as we are informed was neither claimed nor coveted by him. On the contrary, he made little effort to conceal his feelings with respect to it, for he complained bitterly not only as a proprietor who had been despoiled of his possessions, but as a parent who had been robbed of his own fair child, and had been offered in its stead the lean and ill conditioned offspring of another, alien in form, unlike in feature, and different in name, whom he could neither press to his heart nor recognize as his own. The Toronto University was not King's College, either in conception or in result. In those halls for education which he, a christian bishop, had striven to raise, he dreamt not of a perishable home, for the discipline of study, which he had been accustomed to believe ought to be, and which he hoped to see would be carried on there, like the discipline of teaching, which was to be continued elsewhere, was preparatory only. The matriculants in his esteem were heirs of salvation, candidates for immortal honours, for degrees in "the house not made with hands." The school, the college, the university, represented the porch of the Church, and the Church was the vestibule of heaven. They were in his esteem the essential parts of a prescribed pathway through which mortal man might pass from "the city of destruction" to "the Mount of God."

It is possible to imagine, though it is less easy to portray, the bitter trial through which the stricken Bishop must have passed, as one idol after another was crushed at his feet, and scattered beyond his reach. It is true, indeed, that his mind was severely disciplined to disappointment, for the lamp of success had very rarely brightened the pathway of his public life. Yet, even though we make allowance for the fact that he was familiar with failure, it is not easy to analyze the emotions which must have visited him as he took note of the gradual growth of the Toronto University. Even a stranger is struck with the external beauty of that visible representation of applied science. Like a gem of mediæval art, fittingly set in a frame-work of verdure, it silently commands the admiration it receives. But it is not difficult to suppose that to the eye of the Bishop such unquestionable charms rather aggravated than diminished the anguish of his soul. It was hard for him to see such perfection of beauty separated, if not estranged, from the supreme author and source of beauty. It was hard for him to see those brave old trees jubilant with joy, waving their glad arms around those curious carvings and dainty fretworks, and not to feel within his nature a root of bitterness with which they, at least, had no sympathy. It was hard to see such "a fabric huge rise like an exhalation," on the very ground, near to the very spot, which had been prepared and set apart by him for a purpose so similar, and yet so unlike; oh! it was hard to see and not to feel in the overthrow of hope how exquisitely painful is the irony of joy. Moreover, it was impossible for his clear mind to be insensible to the fact, that the noble structure which adorned those college grounds like a jewelled casket was correspondingly rich in its furniture of thought. There was the requisite machinery, including many of the pleasant, and most of the necessary appliances for work, and there, too, were the human parts, the professors and masters singularly well chosen, to control and direct all. Beauty and culture were there, but the untravelled heart of the venerable Bishop yearned for its Christian cloister, for the voice of prayer and the song of praise, for the law and discipline by which learning had been hallowed in the ages of the past. He missed what he deemed to be the pivot of the system, for he saw not the central glory from which all education in his judgment should proceed. He mourned less for the success of his adversaries than for the slight to his church, less for their triumph over him than for the missing Shekinah, the absent altar, and the unoffered morning and evening sacrifice; he mourned, and who shall chide him for his grief, for what he regarded as the virtual eclipse of faith within those walls. Men may make light of creeds, catechisms and confessions of faith, they may sneer at prejudices, discredit motives and ridicule dogma ; nevertheless, the picture of a good man's sorrow is no unworthy subject of contemplation. It is always touching for its sadness, and sometimes eloquent for its sublimity. It sobers the sense, quickens the pulse and touches the soul, for it appeals to our better nature, and reminds us of the goodness from which we have fallen. It is inflamed with the brightness of the better land and acknowledges the excellence of goodness in this. It throbs with virtue, and thrills with immortality, for its yearnings reach from the visible to the everlasting, from "the life that now is, to that which is to come."

But if such reflections disquieted the Bishop they produced no corresponding effect on the minds of those who, with the property, had won the right to control the educational system of the Province. Having opposed the Bishop from considerations of conscience, or motives of policy, such persons were neither required nor expected to feel as he felt, or to be sorrowful as he was. They had been educated according to another rule, and having graduated in a different school of thought they were governed by another principle of action. To them King's College even under its amended charter expressed the triumph of an obnoxious party and the ascendancy of a prelatical church. The amended charter was an offence if not an abomination. The chair of divinity represented ancient dogmas which they discredited, and an ecclesiastical policy that was obnoxious to the Divine Law. They did not sympathize with the objections commonly entertained by English Churchmen to mere clerical seminaries for the education of youth, neither would they see any disadvantage in the separate education of youth intended for holy orders, from the youth intended for secular callings. Having no sympathy with the University system of the mother country they would be no parties to its introduction into Canada. In their judgment, the plan of the Bishop for uniting religious with secular education was embarrassing if not hurtful, and included greater difficulties than it overcame. They, therefore, separated the subject from its accessories, and making light of the argument derivable from sacred obligation as well as from established usage, they regarded the struggle as little more than the effort of an able tactician to secure an advantage to a favoured party. Thus was the question of education and the control of our chief university removed from the privacy and quiet where such work is best carried on into a region of debate and contention, and thus it came to be dealt with, as if it were some political annoyance, such as a boundary or a franchise, the perplexity of one party and the sport of another. In passing, it is difficult to dismiss reflections which are more or less present to the minds of most thoughtful people, for our effort to loose and to bind is by no means free from embarrassing considerations and disquieting fears. One party, for example, destroyed what another party had created, so the institution thus created, proceeding as it does from a parentage of strife, may be said to contain the germ of its own destruction, and therefore in the end may become the prey of all parties. At present, the state purchases forbearance by paying tribute for peace; but let such tribute be withdrawn, let the leash be cut by which fanaticism and self-interest are partially kept in check, then may not the danger arise of an indecent scramble for a desirable property? Canada, in the Toronto University, may possess her Prometheus, and it may, perhaps, be worth while to weigh the cost of unbinding him, for the united forces of local, sectional and religious rivalry, which the myth represents, might perchance fall with fatal impetuosity, if not on the building itself, at least, on the endowments by which it is supported. Such a result would be a national calamity, which no wise man should provoke; but, nevertheless, which might be generated in the lap of political craft and religious exasperation.

The marks of failure which were fatally impressed on the clergy reserve and the university questions, were as indelibly stamped on the Bishop's exertions with respect to common schools. In noting the ill success of those efforts the fact should not be overlooked that the subjects were germain to one another, and that failure in regard to one of them, like an epidemic, might be expected to run its course through the whole. But if there was uniformity in the result, there was also consistency in the plan, for his experience of defeat taught him no new lessons of strategy. In his anxiety to obtain what he deemed to be right, he took no account of what was possible. He aimed at what was absolute and perfect, and rejected what was feasible and mixed. It was contrary to his character to navigate as the sailor steers, he would not veer with the wind or turn as the ship tacks; if he could not keep his course in a direct line he would not attempt to do so by an oblique one, he neither calculated tides nor observed currents, and hence in the opinion of many he failed to touch the haven he might otherwise have reached.

Some persons are of opinion that no religious body in Upper Canada could have exerted more influence than the Anglican Church, in moulding the common school system of that Province; and yet it is probable that no religious body has shewn less aptitude for such work. Those who have spoken for her have pitched their voice to a key unfamiliar to the majority of her members. Such utterances may have been theologically sound, but they were practically inapplicable and positively inexpedient. The Bishop's principles, like his character, were not fashioned in a flexible mould, for they were not made of malleable but of cast iron. He was unbending in purpose and unyielding in action. His opinions were not sentiments but convictions; moral properties of which he deemed himself to bethe trustee, and from which he would not abate one jot or relinquish one tittle. Compromise was foreign to his experience, and concession was unsuited to his temper. Hence he had little respect for their researches, and none for their conclusions who teach that the history of the church of England, like the history of the realm of England, is in fact a history of compromise.

But disappointment did not result in despair. There was dignity as well as grace in the way in which he accepted defeat. Indeed his character never shone to greater advantage than when he snatched a triumph from an overthrow. His resources were as manifold as they were inexhaustible. At the age of seventy-two he ceased from strife, and bowing obediently to a painful law, he began with renewed industry to build afresh what we regard as the fairest, and what we believe will prove to be the most enduring monument to his fame. Sweet to him had been the uses of adversity, for though his contest with the civil power had been obstinate and exhausting, and though he had been worsted in that contest, nevertheless, his ascent from the "valley of humiliation" was luminous, if not with victory, at least with hope. In the strength of acquired wisdom and inherent faith, he appealed to new agencies, and called into use new instruments of work. He took a new survey of the moral landscape, and examined afresh the most approved modes of christian warfare, and he soon learned how to move and combine forces with which, until then, he was presumed to be unfamiliar, and in which he had placed but little trust. Thus it was that by means of what we may truly call "the weak things of the world he confounded the things that were mighty." Turning from princes, in whom he ceased to place his trust, and from laws, which, like reeds had broken beneath his weight, he appealed to sentiment and religion, to faith and duty, to individual sympathy, and to individual sacrifice. In the sacred names of truth and justice, he invoked the aid of that voluntary principle which he had formerly discredited, and sought in the free-will offerings of the many, what he had hoped to find in the munificence of one. He appealed to honour and self-interest, to the recollection of wrongs, and the conviction of right, and his stirring words called into life the latent enthusiasm of gifted souls. His heart was inflamed with the fire he had kindled. He would scarcely give sleep to his eyes, or slumber to his eyelids, until he had erected a college wherein the divine law should fill the chief place in the circle of the sciences. Thus he turned from the creature to the Creator, from human policy to the divine government, from man to God. He shut the statutes that the sunlight might shine upon the gospel. He endeavoured "to forget the things that were behind," that he might, with an untrammelled mind, "reach forward to those that were before," and being impelled by memory and allured by hope, he moderated his appeal to the intellect that he might intensify his address to the heart. It was a brave sight to behold the heroic Bishop playing the roll of a voluntary. It was a brave sight to see one who had passed the period of life allotted by the Psalmist, stooping afresh to take up its burden, and submitting once more to the toils and sacrifices, the trials and disappointments which he had some right to lay aside. It was a brave sight to see one who could be indifferent to personal ease and conventional prudence, to the suggestions of comfort and the seductions of policy, setting himself to the duty of building in Canada a monument such as William of Wykeham erected at Oxford, not only where the the work of education might be begun in the faith of Christ, but where, in the strength of the adorable Trinity, it might be continued and ended to the glory of God.

We have no space to trace the history of King's College, from the time the Royal Charter was granted, to the time when that Charter was revoked by an act of the Legislation of Canada. It must suffice to mention, that on the 1st January, 1850, the act which substituted the University of Toronto for King's College, came into operation, and, that in consequence of such act, the Bishop issued a stirring pastoral, concluding with these emphatic words:—

"I shall not rest satisfied till I have laboured to the utmost to restore the College under a holier and more perfect form. The result is with a higher power, and I may still be doomed to disappointment; but it is God's work and I feel confident that it will be restored, although I may not be the happy instrument to live to behold it. Having done all in my power, I shall acquiesce submissively to the result, whatever it may be, and I shall then, and not till then, consider my mission in this behalf ended."

On the 10th of April, 1850, he left for Great Britain, and on the 4th of November following, he again returned to Toronto. Three days afterwards, the Medical School, in connection with Trinity College was formally opened, and on the 30th of April following, the corner stone of the College was laid by him with becoming ceremony. On the 15th January, in the succeeding year, the College was opened for work, when the venerable Bishop in his touching speech, very feelingly described his emotions "the joy of grief," ending his eloquent address with these words:

"The rising University has been happily named the child of the Church's adversity, because it is the offspring of unexampled oppression—a solitary plant in a thirsty land, which may yet suffer for a season under the frown of those whose duty it is to nourish and protect it. But the God whom we serve brings good out of evil, and makes the wrath of man to praise him. We, therefore, take courage, and feel assured that as He has smiled upon our undertaking thus far, He will bless it to the end. In the meantime, I trust that Trinity College will henceforth be recognized by every lay and clerical Member of our Communion, as the legitimate child of the Church, and entitled to the benefit of their protection and daily prayer."

Thus were the hopes of half a century realized, and the labours of a life brought to a successful close. The attractive Gothic structure which adorns the western portion of Toronto should and we hope will be regarded by the churchmen of Ontario as the most fitting monument to his fame who in life subscribed himself "John by Divine permission first Bishop of Toronto."

We have given in another place as perfect a list as we could obtain of the persons who were educated by the Bishop at the two schools which he kept at Cornwall and Toronto. It may be proper that we should add a list of the matriculants entered on the rolls of the college which he founded; for that list includes the names of men whose careers will influence the character and form part of the future history of Canada.* The two records embrace a period of sixty years of service and they represent the direct and indirect exertion of one man in the cause of education. People will differ in opinion on what constitutes general education, but the least friendly critic will be prepared to admit that the education that the Bishop of Toronto endeavoured to impart was intended to be as pure as truth, and as far reaching as eternity. The heroic Bishop won for his labours the admiration and gratitude of many of his most distinguished contemporaries, and succeeding generations will apportion to his memory some of the "corn land" of the commonwealth. Among his earliest gifts, he contributed, if we are rightly informed, an amount equal to one year's official income, to the endowment fund; and among his latest he be-

* See Appendix No. 2 to this Sketch.

queathed "to his dear College," "the child of his old age," his "joy of grief," as a mark of affection, the valuable library he had accumulated and the costly plate which his Cornwall scholars had given to him. It is true indeed that many others have, and probably many more will in time to come, by gifts or bequests, or both, wreathe their names with his in fame; nevertheless such contributions will but represent tribute offered to the value of his labours as well as to the purity of his aims. The race of men is by no means extinct who firmly believe that the ancient union of religious with secular education ought not to be put asunder, and that the University which resents and abjures this species of intellectual divorce, ought to receive the alms as well as the prayers of the faithful. Through good report and through evil report, at all times and under all circumstances, in prosperity and in adversity the first Bishop of Toronto was the steadfast and unwearying advocate of the union of religious with secular education. Trinity College is the witness to the earnestness of his vows as well as to the strength of his will. Better than "sculptured urn" or "monumental bust," it represents the crown of his policy and the climax of his faith. We read the confession of the indomitable Bishop as plainly in those walls as if it had been chiselled in the stones whereof they are built: "I believe that God in all things should be glorified."

Bishop Strachan has rested from his labours, but the work which was religiously begun for the glory of God will be reverently continued for the good of man. To future generations Trinity College will possibly represent a Bishop's shrine, where the weary in well doing may renew their strength, where truth may light her torch afresh, where duty may see an example and make a study, and where faith and works, the twin sisters of religion, shall harmoniously exclaim:

> The beauty of a life well spent
> Is his majestic monument

Chapter Third.

As was said of old: If the Lord be God serve Him, but if Baal, then serve him, so it should now be said to the English people, if there be no conscience, no function of religious discernment in well ordered States and if unity in the body be no law of the Church, let us freely abandon the ancient policy under which this land has consolidated her strength and matured her happiness and carried a fame yet wider than the Dominions that are washed by every sea; but if the reverse of both these propositions be true, then let us decline to purchase moral debility and death wrapped in thin disguise and entitled peace, then in the same name of God "to the utmost and to the latest of our power let us steadily abide by the noble tradition of our fathers, and be faithful to posterity even as antiquity has been faithful towards us."

The State in its relations with the Church, by W. E. GLADSTONE, ESQ.; *Fourth Edition*.

IN 1839 the great purpose for which three successive Bishops made tedious and repeated voyages across the Atlantic to accomplish was attained. The diocese of Quebec was divided and the Honourable and Right Reverend John Strachan, D.D., LL.D., was preferred to that portion of it which was erected into the See of Toronto. Subsequently he was consecrated by the Archbishop of Canterbury. The division of the diocese took place when the Act for the re-union of the Provinces of Upper and Lower Canada was under discussion. Though introduced by the Government which had, as we conjectured, authorized his appointment, that act received the uncompromising opposition of the new bishop. He considered it unjust in its bearing upon the church and unwise in its relation to the state, for he was of opinion that the interests of the reformed faith generally and the interests of the protestant inhabitants of Upper Canada in particular, had been sacrificed to the political requirements of the Lower Province.

The Session of the Upper Canada Parliament, which commenced on the third of December, 1839, was the last Session of the Parliament of that Province. The Bishop attended the sittings of that Session as he had done those of previous ones with scrupulous regularity. On the thirteenth of December, the resolutions, on which the Union Act was subsequently based, were agreed to, and on the day following several Protests were entered on the Journals of the Legislative Council including one by the Bishop, where the signature "John Toronto" is first seen in the records of Parliament.

The Protest contains three clauses, but the ecclesiastical points raised were two only. The first, that the Union of the Provinces would prove injurious to the Protestant population as it would place it under a Legislature virtually Roman Catholic; and the second, that the Clergy Reserve question had not previously been settled.

The last time the signature "John Toronto," is to be found in the Journals, occurs on the twenty-first of January, 1840, where his protest is entered against the passing of the Bill, entitled "An Act to provide for the sale of the Clergy Reserves, and for the distributions of the proceeds thereof." Length of time, much discussion and an elaborate correspondence had neither shaken the Bishop's opinions, nor softened his phraseology. He protested in emphatic words, that the Bill was to be deprecated "because it is anti-christian in principle." It fosters "religious divisions," it promotes "indifference to truth" and it "leads directly to infidelity." "It is subversive of the constitution," for parenthetically he adds: "an Established Church is part and parcel of the Constitution of Great Britain and Ireland, and all the dependencies." Therefore "it deprives the Established Church of three fourths of her acknowledged property." It renders the Clergy "stipendiaries of the State," and reduces them to an equality with "unauthorized teachers," thus "violating one of the most sacred doctrines of the Catholic Church." It "admits the Roman Catholics along with the other denominations as sharers in a provision, solemnly set apart for the maintenance of a Protestant Clergy." It "makes the monstrous attempt of constituting seventeen or eighteen religious establishments in one, and the same province," and "it stands without a parallel for its reckless injustice, and irreligious tendencies in the annals of Christian legislation."

In sea phrase, the Bishop in early life had nailed his colours to the mast, and his determination, therefore, was natural enough to go down with his flags flying and his guns run out. That Protest is his last recorded Parliamentary utterance, and so far as the language is the measure of strength, we think it was about his strongest. Indeed it is more remarkable for its force, than for its exactness, for while it displays the intensity of his feelings, it does not, to the same degree, exhibit the accuracy of his reason. The syren like suggestions of prudence could not at that time still the tempest of his passion. It seemed that he must speak or die, and what he had said in the beginning, he would continue to say to the end of his career. He had neither "ratted" nor wavered in his opinions. To him it was the old issue which admitted of no compromise: "If the Lord be God, serve Him, but if Baal, then serve him." Nevertheless the vigour of his vocabulary was by no means exhausted in the phrases of that protest. About fifteen years later, on the 1st of October, 1854, the Bishop addressed a remarkable letter to the Hon. A. N. Morin, who was at that time the leading member of administration from Lower Canada. In that letter the question of settling the Clergy Reserves difficulty, was thoughtfully dealt with and forcibly put. Mr. Morin was a quiet and devout Roman Catholic gentleman, who, from taste and policy, generally expressed what he had to say in gentle language. Moreover he possessed a cultivated mind, and an extensive acquaintance with political as well as with general literature. His experience and research had made him tolerably familiar with the style in which State papers are written, and therefore he knew that diplomats, of the highest school, almost invariably clothed their strongest arguments in the language of gentleness and courtesy.

We have little doubt that Mr. Morin received the Bishop's letter with respect, and we have none that he read it with attention. It is also probable that he was by no means insensible to the force of the Bishop's arguments. But what he did, or how he acted, when he came to the postscript must be imagined by those who have read it and who were acquainted with him. The letter, like a bee, was compounded of honey and sting; but the postscript, like a wasp, was wholly remarkable for the latter. It appears that, after writing and before sending the letter, the Bishop received a copy of the proposed act for what His Lordship termed "the confiscation of the Clergy Reserves." He had struggled manfully for nearly fifty years to avert the evil which was about to fall on his beloved Church. We may therefore well excuse the travail and anguish of his soul as he saw and felt that his hopes were broken, crushed, and scattered like macadamised granite on the common highway. Love's labour was literally lost, and the brave old man stood bereft and beaten, but calmly resolute to the last. As the curtain fell on the drama of his exertion and his failure, many may have said involuntarily: "This was the noblest Roman of them all." If forty years of strife were to be followed by the complete alienation of the possessions which gave rise to the strife, "the old man eloquent" was at all events bent on being faithful unto death and of saying a last word in his own way. Though the adversary might spoil he could not silence him. The impassioned words of Mr. Gladstone with which we have prefaced this chapter may have given direction to the Bishop's thoughts, but they did not govern the language of his remonstrance. The latter is all aglow with heat and anger, with reproach and menace. The Bill says the incensed Bishop is "an atrocious specimen of oppressive legislature." It "is a monstrous robbery" designed by "its silent and venomous operation to undermine and destroy every Parish and Mission in the Diocese." Mr. Morin is asked whether he and his friends are not already "gloating in the prospect of the Anglican Church in ruins." Whether "they are not already rejoicing in the hope that the voice of prayer and praise, and the preaching of the Gospel, will soon cease to be heard in Upper Canada." His Lordship finished his letter with an inquiry, in the nature of a prediction, for he asked whether a taste of spoil would not beget a relish for spoil, and whether in such a contingency the property of the Roman Catholic Church would be sacred against assaults." Thus his earliest convictions on the sacredness of Church property continued to the last, for he closed his political career in words which for sting and strength do no discredit to the acrid style in which theologians too frequently discuss the charities of religion. In passing we may observe that Clerical colloquies make one nervous on the subject of Church Courts, for however much such tribunals, in the opinion of some persons, may be considered desirable, there are, we are inclined to think, very few who would not elect to be tried by a lay, rather than by an ecclesiastical judge.

But after all, it is not easy to suffer and be kind, and it is not necessary to suffer and be silent. Though a cause is rarely promoted by hard words, an individual is not unfrequently relieved by using them, and it is possible that Dr. Strachan experienced this kind of relief when he fired his farewell shot at the Legislature and Parliament of Canada. Like the patriarch of Idumea he occasionally may have been inclined to "curse his day" for the objects for which, as a politician and a churchman, he had striven with heroic fortitude, and around which he had entwined his hopes and his affections, seemed one after another to perish or to elude him. Almost all the important measures which he had opposed as a statesman have been enacted by statesmen who succeeded him, and what must have been more trying to him, was, that almost all the important changes he had resisted as a Churchman have by means of, and through the co-operation of churchmen, been brought to pass.

He had stood aloof in 1846 and withheld assistance from the only plan for a common school of education system that seemed to be either feasible, or possible; and in 1850 the people unfortunately answered him by withholding their sympathy from his plan of higher education, by destroying the university which he had been at so much pains to establish. Again the Bishop thoroughly believed, and sought to make his belief contagious, that the Anglican Church was the established Church of Canada. The people generally not only received his opinion with incredulity and trampled it under foot, but they supplemented their dissent by alienating what was left of the Church lands. This final act admonished all who had theretofore been embarrassed with doubts on the subject, that the Legislature of Canada would neither tolerate a state Church nor sanction a privileged Clergy. Such rebuffs were somewhat rudely given and undoubtedly were hard to bear; but while they justified some reproaches, they scarcely excused the language in which such reproaches were expressed.

Though nearer eighty than seventy years of age, the Bishop's heart was most sensitive to pain, for it had not yet become as "dry as summer's dust." Hence the operation which his latest state paper represented of shaking dust on those who had wounded him and weakened his Church, was not a natural but a painful operation. Though resistance may lessen the power it does not generally alter the character of a man. The peculiarities which had distinguished Dr. Strachan as a politician were not likely to disappear when he was called upon to discharge the office of a Bishop. The refined humility of his saintly contemporary, the Bishop of Quebec, was not the quality by which "John Toronto" was careful to be recognized. On the contrary, he was accustomed to observe that a ruler of the Church, like other men in inferior stations, needed the "wisdom of the serpent as well as the harmlessness of the dove." Neither did the high bred sagacity of the Metropolitan, the Bishop of Montreal, move him to imitation. Indifference was a quality which the Bishop of Toronto could neither affect nor appreciate, for his character was positive and his taste disputatious. He possessed strong feelings, strong affections, and strong prejudices, and his practice was to invoke the aid of his will and to win or to lose with the strong hand. Not unfrequently he found it difficult to be "courteous," and the apostolical injunction of being "all things to all men" was one which he understood less perfectly than he might have done. While possessing much of the heartiness, and many of the aversions, of a Tory, he had little of the softness, and none of the subtleness, of a Whig. He had, for example, some respect but no admiration for the Presbyterian type of christianity. To such of his friends and acquaintances who were members of the Scotch Church his apparently playful but really serious interrogatory was generally expressed in the same words, "And have you not by this time purged yourself of the heresy of John Knox?" He had almost a "Johnsonian" distrust of non-conformists, and occasionally he found it as difficult to observe a conciliatory demeanour towards them as he had formerly found it to show magnanimity towards his political opponents. The theory of "a church by law established" was very grateful to him; for though he loved the Church he doated on the establishment, and, like Lord Eldon, he occasionally used the terms indifferently, as if they expressed the same meaning; for besides the historical and catholic character of its blessings, an established Church represented to him some sublimary and local advantages which he was by no means inclined to surrender. In England, for example, the clergy are a privileged order, and enjoy some political and many social advantages that are not extended to those whom Dr. Strachan was accustomed to describe as "unauthorized teachers." A legal status for the establishment included a social status for the clergy, and both were deemed to be objects especially worthy of preservation. Unfortunately they were struggled for to the prejudice of the order for which the struggle was made, for class privileges, even when they rest on a law basis, very generally irritate the classes that are excluded from such privileges. Moreover, their possession is not unfrequently attended with hurt to those for whose benefit they are claimed. For when such privileges are disputed as matters of fact, or when they possess a doubtful existence in law, the assumption of them is injurious, not only to the cause but to the individuals for whom such assumption is sought. The Church, which was meant for mankind, is apt to shrink into the dimensions of a sect when the status of her rulers is adjusted according to a mere worldly or statutory standard, and moreover, such rulers run much risk of forfeiting social consideration by claiming, as matters of right, privileges that would generally be conceded were no such claims preferred.

In the earlier as well as in the comparatively recent history of

the parent state, ecclesiastics have discharged the duties of statesmen.
Therefore the union in the same person of sacred and secular offices
was not contrary to the constitution of England; and as Canada
is said to possess the "image and transcript of that constitution,"
the like usage may have been considered permissible here. As we
have elsewhere said, the Bishop became a politician in spite of himself,
but having accepted the duties, he was too bold a man to decline
the responsibilities which those duties imposed. So far as Upper
Canada was concerned, the spiritual and temporal powers of the
government were virtually represented in his person, and therefore it
is probable that he was no inattentive student of the careers of men of
his own cloth, upon whom had devolved duties similar to those he
was required to discharge. Necessity, as well as inclination, obliged
him to attach adherents to his views and supporters to his cause,
and thus, as a matter of course, he became not only the leader of
a party but necessarily a partizan. No one will respect his character the
less because he sought to attain his ends by the means, and with the
assistance, of educated and disciplined associates. Such means, under our
present constitution, are considered laudable as well as legitimate, and
may not be overlooked by those who would rule with success; but
when ministerial responsibility was a question of dispute and not
a principle of controul, it was necessary to success that the chief
provincial adviser of the sovereign should be backed by a following
respectable for merit if not for number, for social influence if not for
popular sympathy. But what is cause for regret, and probably was the

occasion of loss, is that Dr. Strachan's policy in matters ecclesiastical was less characterized by a gentle wisdom than by a strong will. It was rather obstinate than dignified, and such obstinacy too frequently degenerated into scolding, accompanied with imputations as to the motives of his opponents, which, whether true or otherwise, ought not have been expressed. Less heat and a more generous appreciation of the difficulties of rulers, as well as of the law of the case, might, and we believe would, on several occasions, have led to happier results. The doubt, for example, as to the legal existence of the establishment in Canada was practically resolved in the negative by Earl Bathurst. It would therefore have been wise at that day to have bowed gracefully to an unwelcome decree, to have thrown the political paraphernalia, which the establishment represents, overboard, and, in a generous spirit, to have come to terms with the Church of Scotland. Had such a course been pursued, the latter church would not have found it necessary to "make to herself friends of the mammon of unrighteousness," and much property would have been saved to both churches that is now irrevocably lost to the sacred cause of the reformed faith. Moreover, the magnanimity of the act would have commanded respect, and might, perhaps, have secured the adhesion of many to the Anglican Church who are now, it is to be feared, almost hopelessly estranged from her communion. At all events, the political and party character, which has done so much to discredit the spiritual character and narrow the influence of the Anglican Church, would have been got rid of, and she would have secured the attachment of some who, like Cobden, for example, found the liberality of his principles in some sort reflected in the liberality of her system. Unhappily, men of advanced opinions were, for the most part, routed and expelled from her communion by the exaggerated partizanship of the clergy, and by the illiberal aspersions of the laity.

In his intercourse with the clergy, the Bishop, almost invariably, was kind and generous, considerate and just; hence he was regarded by them with affection as well as respect. His reverence for authority inclined him to support authority, and therefore his sympathies were generally found on the side of the clergy when any issue was joined between them and their parishioners. Now and then, when the dispute was tangled and knotted by temper or feeling, he shewed the tact which Napoleon was accustomed to display, by complimenting the officer and removing him to another command. Not only was the Bishop a "Father in God" by his office, but he was by habit and experience inclined, on all seasonable occasions, to display the attributes of paternity. When, for example, he saw fit to admonish "a brother," or to rebuke "an elder," or to give a synod a piece of his mind, it was done in a fatherly way; that is, sententiously, and to the point, and a very sharp point it was, as many can testify who felt its pungency. It is true, indeed, that like ordinary parents when moved to anger by unruly children he was sometimes arrogant and sometimes menacing, occasionally supercilious, and, considering that he was dealing with men and not with boys, it must be allowed that he too frequently feathered his contempt with what could scarcely be distinguished from rudeness. The order "Sit doon, sir, ye're talking nonsense," * was uttered by one, who, according to the Rev. Dr. Scadding, could give to vowels and diphthongs a North British depth and breadth.

> "Mouthing out hollow o's and a's,
> Deep-chested music."

"The Rhætian tones" which appear to have soothed the ear and to have won the smile of Dr. Scadding require to be understood to be appreciated. Nevertheless it is agreeable to find one of the Doctor's critical taste and acoustic accuracy saying not only a kindly word for the "hollow o's and a's" that in his innocence were supposed by the writer to have been the difficulty of all who had not had the good fortune to have been born on the north-side of the Tweed, but actually wreathing about their rugged homeliness a web of rhetorical fascination as charming to see as it is difficult to appreciate. Such eulogy administers a rebuke while it provokes envy. When the writer remembers how much effort he made in years gone by to separate the "o's and a's" from the words they massacred, he feels very humble in the presence of Dr. Scadding's criticism, and very jealous of the Doctor's listening and descriptive powers. Apart, however, from the advantage of the order "Sit doon, sir, ye're talking nonsense," being expressed with the accompaniment of "deep chested music;" stripping it of the poetical investiture and lyrical accompaniments with which an instructed fancy has clothed it, and receiving it as an expression of simple English, the

---

* The first Bishop of Toronto, Review and Study by Henry Scadding, D.D., Cantab.

plain words must be regarded as objectionable as well as irregular for the purpose for which they were used. In point of fact the interval which separated the Bishop from the Master of the Cornwall School was forgotten, and the dignity which belongs to the former office was substituted for the energy that characterized the latter. For example, it was the master of the fourth form giving an imposition to a boy, rather than the Bishop of a Diocese rebuking a man, when in answer to the deferential remark of a speaker, addressing an audience over which the Bishop was presiding, on some point of order, "that he was in the hands of the meeting," was roundly informed in "Rhætian tones," such as Ossian might have used, "Nae, nae, ye're not, ye're in my hands; sit doon, sir."

Such energy provoked smiles and perhaps facilitated business, but it did little more, for mirth and speed may occasionally be obtained at too great a cost. In extenuation it should be borne in mind that the theatre of the Bishop's political and ecclesiastical exploits was what in England would be called a Transatlantic one, and hence his style in controversy would also be Transatlantic, somewhat strong, and very decided, clearly aggressive and distinctly menacing. Nor should it be overlooked that the country was actually new, and morally small, and we have the testimony of the Honourable Joseph Howe, confirmed by Sir John A. Macdonald, to the fact that, to modify their figure, "the smaller the pit the harder the fight." Indeed experience teaches that young communities like young persons are apt to follow the guidance of their will, since they have chiefly to rely on the force of that quality for their success. Hence they express their sentiments in language more remarkable for strength than for polish, more conspicuous for force than for courtesy. The hammer of Thor, as a weapon, is preferred to the lancet of Esculapius. The *tu quoque* style of argument, which is frequent in Municipal bodies, and occasional in Legislature ones, sometimes creeps into more serious courts and blemishes more solemn tribunals. In one case it speaks out of the ermine of a judge and in another it whispers in the lawn of a bishop. Nevertheless, the subject of this paper, notwithstanding his peculiarities and in spite of his contradictions, was magnanimous as well as courageous; and magnanimity and courage, like forbearance and charity, represent many virtues while they atone for a multitude of faults.

The Bishop's views were large views, and when they could be advanced without violence to his religious logic, they were generous views. Thus, in his dealings with his clergy, he recognized great latitude of opinion, for practically he had a fair appreciation of the religious liberty which is consistent with the spirit and genius of the English race and the English Church. His own principles were clear and well defined; nevertheless he had a scholar's respect for the learning as well as for the principles of other people, and hence he neither required an Islington pass-word nor a Liturgical shibboleth from clergymen who desired to work in his diocese. In common with the great body of Anglicans he may have preferred the principles of Arminius to those of Calvin, but he did not on that account brand with an anathema, or blemish with a prejudice, those weaker Christians who are not able to receive the full measure of the Catholic faith. It is probable that the Bishop was not indifferent to the general belief that moral goodness lies at the root of all religion and that personal virtue is its best expression. Some modern preachers are confessedly too apt to treat the Gospel as a system of theology rather than as a rule of life. One of Dr. Strachan's curates in years gone by was, it is said, accustomed to teach in this one-sided way. In tones as entirely unexceptional as they were accurately balanced, the curate in question was in the habit of publicly analyzing doctrines that he had privately dislocated, until the mind of the listener became a maze of theological phrases, whose spiritual value was made to depend on emotional considerations which his heart, probably, had not experienced, or on theological ones which his intellect, possibly, could not reach. After such a sermon Dr. Strachan is reported to have said to the preacher, "my young friend, you have only preached half the Gospel this morning, I must preach the other half this afternoon." Unfortunately, the afternoon sermon was so heavily charged with "deep chested music" that the advantage that should have attended the delivery was, we are afraid, less complete than it certainly would have been had the dialect been more English and less "Rhætian."

The Bishop, with the co-operation of his parishioners, built and rebuilt the Parish Church of Toronto four times, and on each successive occasion at increased cost and with augmented beauty. The present church is a large and imposing structure, and when the interior arrangements are altered and better suited to the purposes of worship, the building will not be ill adapted for cathedral services. The Bishop's fame will survive in his works. He co-operated in the establishment of many philanthropic and benevolent associations. He founded two universities and one college for the education of youth. If we are not misinformed, it was he who originated the church society of the diocese, and furthered by example, as well as by precept, the mission work of that important organization. He held the first Diocesan Synod that was convened in Canada and thoroughly concurred in the canons agreed to at Quebec for the creation of a Metropolitical See and for holding Provincial Synods. He initiated the sustentation fund for the support of his clergy, as, in addition to the freewill offerings of the laity, he desired to secure for every minister of his church a moderate endowment;* and furthermore it was he who promoted, if he did not initiate, the plan of setting apart public cemeteries for the burial of the dead.

In his *Bibliotheca Canadensis*, Mr. Morgan mentions that in the year 1811, under the signature of "Reckoner," the Bishop wrote no less than seventy essays in the *Kingston Gazette*. It would gratify the curiosity of many, and be interesting to all, could we only give the titles of those essays; but alas! we have neither the facts nor the space for such a recital. There can be no doubt that he was a voluminous as well as a vigorous writer. The subjects of his pen included sermons and tracts; biographical, historical and statistical papers; letters on political, theological and ecclesiastical subjects; charges to his clergy, journals of his visitations, and pastoral letters to his Diocese. He was a healthy scribe, and a keen disputant, for he relished controversy. "The waters

---

* For list of clergymen ordained by the Bishop of Toronto see Appendix No 3 to this sketch.

of strife" were not distasteful to him, for he was accustomed to dare them; neither was opposition without compensating advantages, since it called into exercise the "native hue of his resolution." His sacred office and the claims of his cloth generally served to tone his language, and keep his temper in subjection to his will, yet, as we have elsewhere said, the "old Adam" would occasionally shew itself in the form of sharp set words; for when, like the late President Lincoln, "he put his foot down," the muscular exploit was occasionally attended with some perceptible consequences, including abrasions to courtesy, bruises to charity, and damage to the pride, if not to the argument, of the assailant. But, though there was a sting in his style, there was no spite in his nature. He might throw his antagonist roughly, but he would pick him up again kindly. Or, should the issue of the conflict be reversed, he would accept his defeat with the grace of one who could respect his victor.

The benevolence of the Bishop was practiced with systematic and discriminating gracefulness. Misfortune rarely appealed to him in vain, and poverty seldom left his house unrelieved; for compassion and charity were as conspicuous in his character as fidelity and endurance. With respect to projects connected with religion, his liberality was a proverb. There were few churches or parsonages in the Province in regard to which the striking imagery of the Prophet Habakkuk could not have been applied, for "the stone might have cried out of the wall," and "the beam out of the timber might have answered it," and each have told the other that its presence there was due to the silver or the gold which were his gifts. Money with him was apparently regarded as nothing more than a talent to be used, as a trust to be administered. He loved it not for its own sake, and no surprise was expressed that he saved little and died poor.

In matters of charity and benevolence, as well as in matters of general philanthropy or local improvement, his were the sagacious counsels and the strengthening words, the guiding hand and the generous heart, the advice and co-operation that went far towards crowning exertion with success. Moreover, there was a phase of charity which shewed itself conspicuously in those exacting forms of civic courage which test our metal, and are perhaps more trying to personal endurance than any act of physical daring. "The pestilence that walketh in darkness, and the destruction that wasteth in the noon-day" represent shapes of evil, before which brave men have quailed, and from which even valiant men have fled. But such terrors wrought no perceptible change in him. His holy faith and his sacred calling nerved him with strength, and both were harmoniously exhibited in his works. In fulfilling the duties which seemed to lie in his path, he was not accustomed to take thought of consequences. He believed that He who "considered the lilies" would not overlook him. In the fearful cholera seasons of 1832-34, his well-remembered figure seemed to be ever abroad, for the only difference he made was to redouble his exertions, and stick closer to his duty. In thus confronting danger with a Christian man's courage, he reproached no one, while his example put many to shame, for he calmly discharged services from which they who ought to have performed them shrank with dismay. Having visited the sick, and prayed with the dying, he was frequently obliged to shroud the dead, to place them with his own hands in hurriedly made coffins, and bury them in hastily made graves. As a good citizen, as well as a laborious minister, he endeavoured to practice what he preached. Religion with him was less a sentiment than a duty, and thus the pathway of his long life was less beautified with the blossoms than strewn with the fruits of benevolence. He did not seem to age in his tastes or his occupations. His memory kept green long after the memories of his contemporaries became seared and yellow. Youth always attracted him, and his affections turned with especial fondness toward little children, not only because they were the best human types of purity and innocence, but because their natures were bright and hopeful like his own. Many will remember with what unalloyed happiness he adapted his conversation to their capacity, as well as the exuberant joy with which his presence was looked forward to and greeted by them. He knew how to combine the offices of a Bishop and a friend, and he set no light value on the influence for good which might be exerted by one who could, in his life and conversation, shew the truth of the Psalmist's experience, that the ways of religion are "ways of pleasantness, and that all her paths are peace."

But the period was fast approaching when he was to close his eyes on the scenes of his toil and his fame. The hand of time, it is true, was laid with rare gentleness on him, but he was not insensible to its pressure. The duties which he had theretofore been enabled to perform without difficulty became exacting and oppressive. His conscience rebelled against the intermission of any of those duties, and hence arose his desire for relief and assistance. The Diocesan Synod appreciated his wish, and interpreted it aright when they elected as his coadjutor in the Episcopate, one who had been his pupil and was his friend, who had shared his thoughts and sympathized in his plans, and with whom he could confer with confidence, and act with affection. In 1866 the Venerable A. N. Bethune, D.D., and archdeacon of York, was duly elected to the office, and in virtue of canons, passed by the Synod in the previous year, he was, on the 25th January, 1867, on the Festival of St. Paul, consecrated as the Bishop of Niagara, with an understanding that he should eventually succeed to the See of Toronto.

The year which opened thus suggestively, was destined ere its close to fulfil the purpose for which its solemnities had made provision. The season of flowers, fruits and golden sheaves had passed away. "The chaplet of the year" had faded, and the "angry winds" of winter were ready to issue from their icy caves. The Autumn Festival of All Saints, the last in the annual cycle of the Church Services, the "drear November day" arrived, when the venerable Prelate, for whom an assistant had been chosen, was to be separated from the cares of his Bishopric; and his soul, with "the souls of the righteous," was to pass "the hand of God," where "no torment shall touch them,"

> To soar those elder Saints to meet
> Gather'd long since at Jesus feet.

Notwithstanding his respect for, and possibly his envy of, those good Christian people whose holy faith is so attractively confident and so actually etherial that it can mount, eagle-like, and at once, from the depths of the human soul to the heights of the New Jerusalem, the Bishop cultivated a tender and sympathetic regard for the larger number of less exalted and more infirm believers, who can only move with slow and measured steps towards "the City of the Great King," who require steps to the altar and need supports by the way; "a rod and a staff," perchance wherewith to tread "the delectable land," and a leading hand that they may climb with safety the starry heights beyond. Such pilgrims won the Bishop's loving regard. He sympathized with them in their desire for sympathy; he appreciated their thirst for fellowship, and he commended their human efforts to lead a devout life. Learn to live aright if men would learn to die aright; such was the Bishop's counsel; use such aids to holy living as holy seasons afford, as holy men of old have consecrated by their lives and by their examples to help and to stay, to solace and to support, "the weary and the heavy laden" in their perilous journey to "the distant hills." The Christian year represented to him a cycle of sacred monitors, whose offices were designed to teach men "how to live that they may dread the grave as little as their bed."

Hence it was that, by precept and by example, the Bishop taught men reverently to observe the appointed fasts and festivals of the Church, and it will occasion no surprise to learn that he, who thus taught, solemnly marked such days for religious and holy worship. This law of his conscience and of his church was strikingly exemplified in the sermons carefully prepared by him for such occasions. It is true that the congregations to which those sermons were delivered were censurably and unaccountably small, nevertheless he took no note of numbers, for his discourses were as thoughtfully written for the "two or three" who then met together, as they would have been for a full congregation of worshippers. Such a practice sprang from a sense of duty, and not from a hope of applause, for the alloy of human ambition found no place in his religious services. The ladder of pride was not the means by which he was instructed to reach the dwelling place of the Most High.

> THOU art mighty; we are lowly;
> Let us reach THEE, climbing slowly,

was his confession and his practice. "Let us reach Thee," if not altogether at least one by one. "Let us reach Thee," for

> Thou shalt redeem us one by one,
> Where'er the world encircling sun
> Shall see us meekly kneel.

In speaking of preaching and public worship we must not omit to notice a circumstance to which Canon Dixon has referred with natural admiration. It would appear that the last sermon the Bishop delivered was singularly solemn in its lesson, and as the event showed, almost prophetic in its application. Like love in death the discourse was laden with memory and hope, with experience and anticipation.

> Love brightens backward through the past,
>   And gilds the stormy path he trod,
> And forward, till it fades at last,
>   In light, before the feet of God.

Heart, soul and lips, the sympathetic triad, seemed to answer one another, for they were "beauty laden" with the passionate language of adoration. In the words of a holy Apostle the aged Bishop in the closing words of his last sermon exclaimed with unwonted fervour: "I am persuaded that neither death, nor life, nor angels, nor principalities, nor powers, nor things present, nor things to come, nor height, nor depth, nor any other creature, shall be able to separate us from the love of God, which is in Christ Jesus our Lord."

He who spake thus had nearly reached the age of fourscore years and ten; and although his physical powers had very perceptibly given way, the serene sunshine of intellect still lingered about his head, for his mind continued bright and clear to the last. The frail body was manifestly hastening towards earth, while the aspiring soul, peradventure, was beating the bars of its prison house, and struggling towards heaven. It was seemly that the festival of "All Saints," the festival which the Anglican Church holds in especial reverence, should have been the day whereon he was to pass through the grave and gate of death, to his reward and his rest, to his consolation and his crown, to the congregation of those who in the portion of scripture appointed for the Epistle for the day are represented as "standing before the throne and the Lamb, clothed with white robes and palms in their hands." It was the poet's picture reduced to experience. The vision of the saintly Keble shewn in life.

> How quiet shows the woodland scene!
> Each flower and tree, its duty done,
> Reposing in decay serene
> Like weary men when age is won,
> Such calm old age as conscience pure,
> And self-commanding hearts ensure,
> Waiting their summons to the sky,
> Content to live, but not afraid to die.

In a notice on the subject which is to be found in the Journal of Education for Upper Canada, the Reverend Dr. Ryerson very pertinently remarks "that the Bishop had long outlived the jealousy of distinctions and the enmity of parties. He ceased at once to work and live, amid the respect and regrets of all classes of the population." In truth he survived all his early contemporaries, whether friends or enemies. The descendants of the former mingled with their hereditary love great personal admiration, while the removal of the occasions of strife enabled the latter to feel and to confess that there remained enough of what was sterling in his character to entitle him to their respect. No such congregation of mourners had ever before assembled within the walls of that large Cathedral, for almost the whole community was stirred by a common grief for a common loss. Many loved, all respected him, and not a few were there who had preserved rare morsels of precious memories which, in thought at least, they cast like votive offerings, in the "unveiled bosom" of his "faithful tomb."

The plate on the coffin bore the following inscription:

THE HONOURABLE AND RIGHT REVEREND

JOHN STRACHAN, D.D., LL.D.,

FIRST BISHOP OF TORONTO.

Born 12th April, 1778. Died 1st November, 1867.

The coffin, as we read, was carried to the hearse, and afterwards to the grave, by old pupils of his Toronto school, whose names are among the familiar household names of the Western Province: they were the Venerable Archdeacon Fuller, the Rev. W. MacMurray, D.D., Mr. Vice-Chancellor Spragge, Mr. F. H. Heward, Mr. William Gamble and Mr. John Ridout. The touching service for the burial of the dead was said, the former part by the Rev. Canon Baldwin, A.M., and the latter by the Very Rev. Dean Grasett, B.D. The proper lessons were read by the Rev. Canon Bevan, D.D. The garish light of day was excluded from the building, and the jets of gas were permitted only to gleam with feeble lustre, here and there, amidst the thick drapery of mourning which, pall like, enshrouded the place where he had prayed for more than fifty years. Darkness was indeed made visible, but light enough remained to illumine the silver plate, which, like a luminous hatchment, brightened, while it indicated, the central cabinet of death. Men, perchance, spoke in whispers of the "spirit that's gone," or with becoming reverence of "the mortal that had put on immortality." The breath of the living seemed to rise like incense to Him who had taken to